THE PRACTICE OF THE
PRINCIPLES OF JESUS

THE PRACTICE OF THE PRINCIPLES OF JESUS

BY
WILLIAM P. KING

NASHVILLE, TENN.
COKESBURY PRESS
1926

Copyright, 1926
BY
LAMAR & BARTON

Printed in the United States of America

DEDICATION

To the Social Service Commission of the
Methodist Episcopal Church, South,
and to the Companion of the Par-
sonage, whose life is a daily
expression of the ideals
set forth herein

FOREWORD

In response to the invitation of Dr. Comer M. Woodward of Emory University, the Chairman of the Social Service Commission of our Church, I gave four lectures at the Lake Junaluska Assembly before a group of representative men and women of the Church. This volume is published at the urgent solicitation of this group. The four lectures are elaborated into four chapters, and six other chapters are added with the same general application.

On account of this addition, it is only just to say that this group is not to be held accountable for some ideas advanced with which certain readers may not be in harmony. I wish to express my satisfaction at the reception of the four spoken lectures. I am confident that the motive of the select company who urged the publication of this volume is altogether different from that of Job, when he said, "Oh that mine adversary had written a book." And now that the book is written, I do not think that I should be held under any obligation to read it. It is nothing but fair that others should do this. There should be a division of labor.

For their assistance in preparing the manuscript and in removing some grammatical blemishes and in making other improvements in the language, an expression of gratitude is due Rev. Homer Thompson, Rev. G. L. King, Dr. Comer M. Woodward; and Dr. H. J. Pearce, Jr., of Brenau College. The readers will recognize my indebtedness, which I gratefully acknowledge, to several leading authors. I have not given the names of books from which quotations are taken, since my discussion is not so distinctively controversial that the readers would wish to verify the quotations.

THE AUTHOR.

CONTENTS

	PAGE
FOREWORD	vii
INTRODUCTORY NOTE	xi

CHAPTER

I. FINDING THE FUNDAMENTALS	1
II. THE PRAGMATIC TEST OF CHRISTIAN DOCTRINE	29
III. THE FALLACY OF THE FALSE ALTERNATIVE	53
IV. THE GOLDEN RULE	75
V. THE GOLDEN RULE (*Concluded*)	105
VI. ORTHODOXY AND OBEDIENCE	126
VII. ORTHODOXY AND OBEDIENCE (*Concluded*)	147
VIII. SOCIAL SOLIDARITY	172
IX. THE NEW CRUSADE	190
X. THE NEW CRUSADE (*Concluded*)	219

INTRODUCTORY NOTE

In the present volume Rev. W. P. King has done a very important piece of work. He has placed before us considerations which help us to get and keep our bearings. In the past decade the thought world seems to have been almost completely torn from moorings and anchorages which we had considered unbreakable. To many a storm-tossed mind everything seems to be afloat and adrift. The reader of this book soon discerns that, bad as our plight seems, the essentials of thought and faith have not suffered shipwreck. In the realms of the social attempt to apply the Gospel to present-day conditions especially, it is possible to chart a course not only toward safety, but toward a fairer kingdom of humanity than any we have ever known.

It is difficult for most of us to be prophetic and discriminating at one and the same moment. If we become prophetic, we yield to the glory of the vision before us and cease to consider closely the actual obstacles in our path; and if we proceed with intellectual carefulness we are likely to lose sight of the grandeurs of the sky. The author seems to me to have kept his eyes fixed on a noble ideal and at the same time to have maintained touch with the actual and concrete. He has not loosened his grasp on his fundamentals because of the false antitheses which so sadly perplex the untrained thinker.

FRANCIS J. MCCONNELL,
Bishop of the Methodist Episcopal Church.

THE PROGRAM OF CHRISTIANITY

"And he came to Nazareth, where he had been brought up; and he entered, as his custom was, into the synagogue on the sabbath day, and stood up to read. And there was delivered unto him the book of the prophet Isaiah. And he opened the book, and found the place where it was written:

The Spirit of the Lord is upon me,
Because he anointed me to preach good tidings to the poor;
He hath sent me to proclaim release to the captives,
And recovering of sight to the blind,
To set at liberty them that are bruised,
To proclaim the acceptable year of the Lord."

—*Luke 4:16-19.*

THE PRACTICE OF THE PRINCIPLES OF JESUS

CHAPTER I

FINDING THE FUNDAMENTALS

I

In an effort to reach the great simplicities of the gospel of Jesus Christ we must steer our way between different types of extremists.

There are the radicals and intellectual snobs who sharpen the intellect and cut out the heart.

They are fragmentary men like Wordsworth's

> "One that would peep and botanize
> Upon his mother's grave,
> One to whose smooth-rubbed soul can cling
> Nor form nor feeling, great nor small,
> A reasoning, self-sufficing thing,
> An intellectual all in all."

With this type of man the analytic spirit has become a frenzy, and the love of dissection a morbid passion.

The radical, of whatever kind, who ignores the contribution of the past, the large element of truth in the great creeds of the past, will himself be ignored by the future. The man who fails to connect with the past misses connection with the future. We have representatives of this type of mind who turn all thought into a universal negation.

> "Woe worth the knowledge and bookish lore
> Which makes men mummies,
> Weighs out every grain of that which was miraculous before,
> And sneers the heart down with the scoffing brain."

The opposite type is represented by Fundamentalists who, with all their limitations and defects, are in possession of some qualities which call forth our admiration.

Even the intolerance of Fundamentalists results from the faith that religion is the one thing of supreme value, and they believe it is being taken away from them. My difference is with the leaders of Fundamentalism, who breathe out "threatenings and slaughter," who become expert in making an appeal to popular passion and prejudice, and who become in reality the enemies of the faith as they encumber it with impossible conceptions.

The hurtful error of Fundamentalism is in magnifying the secondary and incidental to a place of importance along with the primary and fundamental.

The Fundamentalists are bound by the utterly senseless principle, "False in one, false in all," which, if we were compelled to accept, would utterly destroy the very foundation of the faith.

A wise teacher gave to a student in religious perplexity over the authorship of the Pentateuch the counsel, "Accept first of all Jesus Christ as your Lord and Master, and when you get to heaven, you can find out about the Pentateuch."

I knew a brother who thought the Christian faith would be gone if the whale did not swallow Jonah, and yet he was opposed to foreign missions. He missed the one fact above all facts that the book of Jonah is intended to teach, and that is the universal compassion of God that could not be limited to the Jewish race. He had a perfect right to believe that the whale swallowed Jonah; but he had no right to allow the whale to swallow not only Jonah, and the reputation of Jonah, but the one lesson of the Book of Jonah.

Such Biblical trifling recalls the incident of some years ago when a university professor stated that Leviticus was mistaken in saying that the hare chewed the cud. The theological uproar was followed by the sage advice:

> "The bishops all have sworn to shed their blood
> To prove 'tis true the hare doth chew the cud;
> O, bishops, doctors, divines, beware,
> Weak is the faith that hangs upon a 'hair.'"

These distinct and contrasted types of extremists must be persistently opposed.

The "New Thought," so called, finds expression in a superstitious supernaturalism. It also finds expression in the elimination of all that is extrahuman.

Dr. S. P. Cadman writes: "Among the rivalries which compete with the Christian pulpit to-day must be numbered those excursions of unlicensed imagination into the unseen known as Theosophy, Christian Science, Mental Healing, and Spiritualism. They are largely the fruits of that revulsion against an overweening materialism which began to assert itself during the later half of the nineteenth century. The exponents of these cults have been quick to detect the longings after the invisible and mysterious, which were discounted even in the Church by the prejudice of liberal clergymen against the Supernatural. Traffickers in its wonders played skillfully upon those longings, which mere reason cannot satisfy nor unbelief quench. Superstition is the worm that exudes from the grave of a buried faith."

Katharine Tynan dwells on the morbidness of cultured people who have abandoned Christianity, and remarks that she has seen the "emancipated" daughter of a bishop swoon because she caught sight of the new moon through glass.

If the Church would save our generation from

the folly and loss resulting from false religious teaching, which more often than not is the more dangerous because of the half truths it embodies, she must repair herself to timely instruction in order to overcome error and fanaticism by a faith luminous with the light divine.

There are those who ignore the past. "And I heard a voice behind me saying." That is the voice of yesterday, and we must hear what the voice says. Dr. J. H. Jowett writes: "There is a prevalent teaching known as the 'New Thought.' I know the literature of this new teaching, and I say that the teaching gives no adequate place of sovereignty to Jesus Christ our Lord. He is not accorded that unique and solitary preëminence which he claims. He is a neglected factor and is left entirely out of the reckoning. And because he is absent other things are missing. I find no mention of guilt. Rarely do I stumble upon the fact of sin. In the New Thought there is no confession of sin, no sob of penitence, no plea for forgiveness, no leaning upon mercy. The atonement is an obsolete device, the pardonable expedient of a primitive day. It is a destructive heresy."

The true prophet, in raising his hearers to new and greater levels of truth and insight, strives to understand the truth already revealed and saturates himself with those immense realities by which men in past ages have lived and conquered. Only in this way can we go forward to new experiences and new discoveries of the truth.

To ignore the inheritance of the faith of our fathers is to impoverish ourselves and our children. To miss connection with the past is to miss connection with the need of the present and future. If we forget the rich achievements of our fathers, we shall in turn be forgotten by our children. There is a continuity of religious thought, and a new faith has no soil in which to grow. The false prophet has an itching desire for novelty, for the sake of novelty. His idea of paradise is to be in the limelight of a public sensation. The dullness of the commonplace palls upon him, even commonplace morals. His chief objection to the Ten Commandments is that they are old.

We can very readily see through the thinness of the pert, shallow type of thinkers who break with the past. But the man who casts everything in the mold of the past and breaks with the present is also a false prophet or following the leadership of false prophets.

Jesus draws a picture of this kind of false prophet, too vivid ever to be forgotten: "Woe unto you, scribes and pharisees, hypocrites! because ye build the tombs of the prophets, and garnish the sepulchers of the righteous and say, 'If we had been in the days of our fathers, we would not have been partakers with them in the blood of the prophets.' . . . Wherefore, behold, I send unto you prophets, and wise men, and scribes; and some of them ye shall kill and crucify; and some of them shall ye scourge in your synagogues, and persecute them from city to city." There has been no lapse in the line of false prophets who raise stones to the prophets of the past, and throw stones at the prophets of the present.

The indiscriminating idolatry of the past is a very easy and cheap affair. It has sufficient truth mixed with error to give it carrying power. This type of mind suffers from farsightedness; or, to use a big word, presbyopia. Greatness can only be seen when it is far off in time. If a man has been dead a sufficient number of years, he becomes a saint; and if he has been dead a still longer time, he becomes infallible. But the passing centuries have no sanctifying effect on a man or a generation. I make no defense of the egotism in the humor of Mark Twain, who represents himself as weeping at the tomb of Adam because Adam did not live in his day and live to see him. But I do not propose to weep because I did not live in Adam's day. Or if I should weep, it would be tears of joy. The righteous and heroic spirits of the past are secure in their achievement, and we have no time to waste in "garnishing their sepulchers."

We shall receive profit more from the spirit than from the letter of their message. We shall be true to our fathers as they were to their fathers, as we make use of some different methods to meet the new need and the new opportunities of our new day.

Some of the most consummate demagogues that it has ever been my displeasure to know were men who glorified the political leaders and the political traditions of a century and more ago. They deal out demagogic drivel. Both political and ecclesiastical demagogues are fond of conjuring with the names of illustrious statesmen and churchmen of the bygone centuries. They know that God has spoken unto the fathers by the prophets, but they expect no fresh message from God for the need of to-day. They would fasten the present as a slave to the chariot wheels of the past.

Jeremiah came into conflict with false prophets of this type, who took as their motto certain words of Isaiah. They won popularity by orthodox phrases and traditional doctrines. They laid hold of Isaiah's words concerning the inviolability of Jerusalem, and the words which were true as spoken by Isaiah became false. According to Jeremiah one unfailing characteristic of the false prophet was in getting his message out of the traditions of the past.

Jeremiah was not a repetition nor imitation

of Isaiah. He was the embodiment of God's will and truth for the generation in which he lived.

The arch heresy, according to Jesus himself, is not in breaking with certain traditions of the past, but in breaking with God's call to meet the duties and opportunities of the present.

> "God fulfills himself in many ways,
> Lest one good custom corrupt the world."

Marcus Dods, in his letters, writes: "I do not envy those who have to fight the battles of Christianity in the twentieth century. Yes, perhaps I do, but it will be a stiff fight. Your very fidelity to the faith will demand courage to think new thoughts, to champion new theories, to proclaim new truths, to live new ideals, to walk with the Master through new Gethsemanes to new Calvaries. The modern prophet with spiritual weapons must needs fight against the mighty forces of reaction and radicalism. He must needs fight again the fight of Paul in beating off the Judaizers with their narrowness on the one hand, and the Gnostics with their false liberality and philosophical looseness on the other. Every day you face a new world. Every day some appendix of functionless creed is removed. Some old tradition goes to the garret; some outworn fabric of dogma is burned to ashes; new scientific discoveries demand new alignments of the faith; new attacks of the enemy demand new weapons of defense; new results of science challenge new adjustments; new social cleavages and groups challenge new translations of the gospel into social values."

There is the advocacy of a narrow sectional and provincial policy.

The advocacy of a policy which promises no constructive effort, which proclaims national aloofness and isolation is against the whole message and spirit of the Christian faith. The old prophets possessed a broad catholicity of spirit. The modern prophet must rise to the spirit of universality.

The world has only advanced through many growing-pains. When we say that false prophets hinder this progress, we do not mean that they are false in that they are depraved in heart, but false in a mistaken judgment.

In the order of the evolution of society it has always been difficult to make the transition from one stage to another. There came a time when the discussion arose in the family as to whether or not it would remain isolated or join with other families into a clan as a matter of protection. There was violent opposition. It was argued that it had never been done before, that the unity of the family would be destroyed.

Then, when the idea was advanced that the clans should combine into a tribe as a safeguard against the attacks of unfriendly clans, the same argument was advanced that it had never been done before, and that it would involve the clan in endless wars.

So when tribes came together in a state and the states into a nation of federated states, there was raised the alarm of dangerous innovation, the destruction of independence and the establishing of a super-government.

As we have reached the stage of development when the whole world is so interrelated as to require a new order of international agreement, we need not wonder that the cry of the obstructionist should be heard in the land.

Kipling has given us the strong lines:

"He knows not England, who only England knows;
He serves not America best, who only America serves."

A belated mind is fatal to large usefulness.

"New occasions teach new duties; time makes ancient good uncouth;
They must upward still and onward who would keep abreast of truth."

There are those who reply to such language with much heat and insist that we do not live in a new world, but in the same old world.

We live in both. We live in an old world with its old sin, with its old human nature, with its old world and old flesh and old devil, with its old gospel, with its old salvation.

We live in a new world with its new scientific knowledge, and new discoveries and new inventions, with its new civilization, with its new problems, with its new duties, with its new complex relationships, with its new international adjustments to be made, and with its new world solidarity.

We are to shake off the shackles of the bondage of traditionalism.

There is the necessity of holding on to the good of the past and going on to the better of the future.

An old man of my acquaintance accepted all innovations that made for his comfort, such as automobiles and electric lights, but stoutly resisted any change in the fatalism of his theology and in his antagonism to Sunday schools and world evangelization.

Dr. Josiah Strong wrote some years ago: "History is strewn with the ruins wrought by political and religious revolutions rendered inevitable by ultraconservatives who could not or would not reconcile themselves to the world's progress, and who restrained and prevented a natural adjustment of institutions to the ceaseless changes of a living and growing civilization."

Bondage to traditionalism is the death of all progress of every kind. If we are only true to the faith as we accept all the beliefs of our fathers, then it must follow that our fathers were not true to the faith, because very fortunately they did not accept all the beliefs of their fathers. In fact, a slavish imitation of the past is a denial of the faith.

We are willing to allow our ancestors to have some voice and some vote, but we are not willing that they should stuff the ballot box.

Sidney Smith, in the "Fallacies of Anti-Reformers," has made some observations, which may be given in brief, and not as a direct quotation.

What shall be said of our wise ancestors and the wisdom of antiquity? With individuals, the oldest has, of course, the most experience, but with generations the reverse is true, and our ancestors who come first are the young people and have the least experience. There has been added to this experience the experience of many centuries. We can claim against our ancestors that we are older than they are in point of the accumulation of experience.

There are so-called irrevocable laws. There is the effort of the dead hand of the past to mold the future.

The sovereign power at any one period can only form a blind guess at the measure which may be necessary at any future period. By the principle of immutable law, the government is transferred from those who are necessarily the best judges of what they want to others who can know little or nothing about the matter.

The sixteenth century decides for the seventeenth, and the seventeenth makes laws for the eighteenth, and the eighteenth dictates to the nineteenth, and the nineteenth states infallibilities for the twentieth. The traditionalists admit that it was wise for every century to make some change from the preceding except our own. Everything has been fixed for us. Those who have least experience make irrevocable laws for those who have the most experience. To suppose that there is anything which a whole nation cannot do which is essential for their welfare and happiness because another generation long ago dead and gone said it must not be done is mere nonsense.

There is the cry of no innovation. To say that all things new are bad is to say that all old things were bad in their commencement. For of all the old things ever seen or heard of, there is not one that was not once new. Whatever is now established was once an innovation. To abuse the new is therefore to abuse the old, since the old was once new. Because a certain thing was good in its day is no convincing reason that it is good in our day. The world is shaken, not only that old things may pass away, but also that new things may appear.

II

There are certain transitional and transforming forces which have borne down on the life and thought of our age with an irresistible impact, and which have made change and readjustment inevitable.

1. There is the new science, with its knowledge of nature, its power over nature, and the scientific method of thought. There has been a marvelous increase in knowledge, and a marvelous application of scientific knowledge to the practical uses of the world. But of still vaster importance is the scientific method of thought, which begins with observation of facts in the construction of a theory, rather than dogmatically assuming a theory and endeavoring to make the facts fit the theory.

2. The scientific spirit compelled philosophy to revise her *a priori* methods of thought. Philosophy does not deny the possibility of knowledge, but it recognizes the conditions and limitations of knowledge. An increasing confidence is placed in the verdict of experience, and in the pragmatic test of the workability of a theory as affording evidence of the truthfulness of the theory.

3. The Democratic spirit has a wide and radical application. At bottom it is a question of authority. There is the changing attitude to-

ward all authority, whether sacred or secular. It is seen in the awakening of nations from the sleep of centuries. It is seen in the arousing of the individual to the authority of his own consciousness in the formation of his political and religious belief. With this spirit the individual man refuses to be obsessed by the external authority of creed-makers, and rejects that which does not appeal to his own reason and experience.

4. Historical criticism constitutes a part of the general advance in knowledge, and results in a change of theological thought. It was inevitable that the methods which the great historians were applying with such brilliant results to the histories and early literatures of the ancient world should be applied also to the Sacred Writings.

5. The study of Comparative Religion throws light on many portions of the Sacred Scriptures.

We gain a reliable knowledge of the Scriptures only as we learn something of the neighboring nations, their ideas, customs, and religions. Stories of the fall, the flood, the giving of the law, all have their parallels in other nations. There is a vast difference in spiritual quality and moral purpose.

The study of the ancient monuments with the ancient codes, such as the code of Hammurabi, 2250 B. C., with its points of resemblance to the Mosaic law, is a refutation of the customary

FINDING THE FUNDAMENTALS 17

idea of the absolute originality of the contents of the Old Testament. The supernatural is to be found in the superiority of the Old Testament laws and narratives.

6. There has been the development of what we may call the intellectual conscience or love for the truth. We are convinced that "we cannot please the God of truth with the unclean sacrifice of a falsehood," even though it be offered in the name of religion. As much as modern science may have contributed to this "passion for veracity," yet the Christian draws his first and abiding love for the truth from Him who said, "To this end was I born, and for this cause came I into the world, that I should bear witness unto the truth."

7. There is the new ethical awakening. The moral conscience which was dull to the cruelty and injustice of industrial relationships has become keenly sensitive. This new ethical insight has sifted out as chaff some of the former and even current conceptions of God. The doctrine of divine decrees by which God foreordained a fixed number of men to eternal damnation is now becoming impossible. Certain theories of the atonement which made God willing to accept the punishment of the innocent instead of the guilty are discarded since they make God less good than a good man.

The famous protest of John Stuart Mill was:

"I will call no being good who is not what I mean when I apply that epithet to my fellow men; and if such a being can sentence me to hell for not so calling him, to hell I will go."

The protest of John Wesley was not less emphatic against the old Calvinism: "Your God is my devil."

We are told of a committee who were examining young candidates for the ministry when one stern member of the committee asked: "Are you willing to be damned for the glory of God?" One candidate replied: "Well, no, not exactly; but I am willing that the committee should be."

8. There is a new social conscience as the result of a new social spirit and the ethical awakening. This social conscience is altering political theories, changing industrial methods, and removing our social indifference. Many practices are now considered sinful which a generation ago were regarded as innocent. We hear the wail that conscience is dying out. The human conscience was never so highly developed and sensitive as it is to-day. If our consciences do not reprove us as much as formerly about our inbred sin, they reprove us much more concerning our antisocial sins.

We are getting farther and farther away from the situation described in the incident of the deacon who was arrested by a sanitary inspector for selling unclean milk, and who under the sudden provocation used profane language. His Church disciplined him for his profanity, but regarded as too trivial for notice his violation of sanitary laws which would possibly result in the deaths of scores of infants.

9. The new Science of Psychology, with much of the materialistic bias which belongs to some of the psychologists, has had a sifting effect on the ideas and doctrines of men. The subliminal or subconscious realm of the mind must be reckoned with, but we resolutely reject the theory that the inspiration of prophets and saints is merely the "uprush" from an unconscious or racial memory. The fact is that the prophetic revealers of God's truth were pioneers who brought a message to men that all their personal consciousness, and all the heritage of the past, could not have reached. In many instances the message was so new that the race had never heard it before.

While we may be called upon by psychology to discriminate and attribute to the region of subconsciousness some of the ideas which appear to us, yet we must acknowledge also the "downrush from the superconscious." Bishop Gore has said: "Something has occurred for which only the experience of the prophets and the witness of Christ can account, and without which the moral treasures of human nature would be vastly impoverished."

III

One can readily understand how these transforming and disturbing forces have made necessary a restatement of the eternal essentials and vital certainties of the gospel.

The apostolic age was free in its attitude toward the burden of traditions, and it was clear and fearless in the separation of rudiments from the vital elements of the faith. It is as truly the mission of the Christian teacher to-day to discriminate between the essential and nonessential as it was the mission of the apostles in the first century, even though it seems to be a perilous undertaking.

Of the danger of making concessions at any point we have been warned by the well-worn illustration of the traveler, pursued by hungry wolves, who endeavored to conciliate them by morsels, until he himself made the last savory morsel. There is a strong suspicion of any effort to distinguish the permanent and transient elements of our belief. St. Paul, however, distinguishes between the commandments of the Lord and his own judgment.

It is an easy matter to spin out pious platitudes; it is more difficult and infinitely better to accept facts with an honest and reverent spirit. Any fact is a thought of God and a sacred thing, whether found on the page of nature or of scripture.

There are certain advanced thinkers, so called, who would eliminate, one by one, even the essentials. But it requires neither advancement nor thought to be destructive. That is merely wanton trifling. The men who hold this attitude toward the Christian revelation are guided not by the evidence of historical research and investigation, but solely by the prejudices and presuppositions of their own minds.

Dr. Alexander Maclaren, who certainly has no leaning toward destructive criticism, has said: "A clear recognition between the divine revelation and the vessels in which it is contained, between Christ and creed, between churches and forms of worship, on the one hand, and the everlasting word of God spoken by His Son, on the other, is needful especially in times of such sifting and unsettlement as the present. It will save us from an obstinate conservatism which might read its fate in the decline and disappearance of traditional Judaism and Jewish Christianity."

The slow paralysis that has crept over the faith of many is a result of the confusion of the vital and incidental matters of the faith. To declare the uncertain things as if they had been revealed, is almost as unfortunate as to declare the revealed things as if they were uncertain;

and it is very confusing, producing either intellectual slavery or anarchy.

There are some considerations that will help us in the separation of the accidental from the universal elements of our creed.

We are to recognize that Christ's authoritative teaching is in the realm of the religious and spiritual. To extend the authority of Jesus beyond the spiritual domain into regions scientific, historical, and literary is to destroy his authority, under the pretense of making it absolute. He does not attempt to give any authoritative word either on the science of Biblical criticism or on the physical sciences.

Dr. G. T. Ladd writes: "There is no reason why a Christian student of the Bible should hesitate to look calmly on the imperfect and passing element of the Old Testament ethics and religion; or why he should shrink from making the distinctions necessary to separate these elements from the perfect and eternal Christian truth. Christ has showed him how to make these distinctions. In making them he is not setting up his judgment against that of the holy men of old; he is only using the very truth which the infallible teacher himself revealed in order to appreciate its vast superiority to that taught by the teachers who lived in the inferior and preparatory stages."

This determining principle will enable us to

make the distinction between certitudes and unverifiable dogma and speculation. We know that man is a sinner with the possibility of salvation; but we do not know the precise method of his origin or all about his history, and these problems we must leave to science. We know that Jesus Christ brought life and immortality to light, but we have no detailed picture of the conditions of life in the unseen world.

It is impossible to convict John Wesley of Fundamentalism. His refusal to stickle for the dogma is a thorn in the flesh of Methodist Fundamentalists. "One circumstance is quite peculiar to the people called Methodists; that is the terms upon which any person may be admitted into their society. They do not impose in order to their admission any opinions whatever. Let them hold particular or general redemption, absolute or conditional decrees; let them be Churchmen or Dissenters, Presbyterians or Independents, it is no obstacle. Let them choose one mode of baptism or another, it is no bar to their admission. A Presbyterian may be a Presbyterian still; the Independent or Anabaptist use his own mode of worship. So may the Quaker, and none will contend with him about it. They think and let think. One condition and one only is required—a real desire to save their souls. Where this is, it is enough; they desire no more; they lay stress on nothing else; they ask only, 'Is thy heart herein as my heart? If it be, give me thy hand.'"

There are essential and nonessential, permanent and transient elements in religious thought and belief. We have magnified the transient and passing into an equality with the permanent and abiding. There is much nervous anxiety over the things that pass away. As we fasten our faith on the surface matters, disturbances are bound to come. How can you sing, "How firm a foundation," if your faith foundation is liable to be shaken any morning by a new figure on the uncertain age of the world? I am not so much concerned about the age of the world as about my own age. I am not so much concerned about lines of savage ancestry that lie behind me as about whether the savagery of my own nature is being overcome. Our age has not lost its faith in religion. Man will be religious as long as he is man. Christianity holds within her bosom indestructible elements. There are some things which can never be shaken.

Modern Fundamentalism is a misnomer, since its peculiar features are not fundamental.

We should be content to find in the Bible an inspired authority in the realm of life and faith. In Jesus Christ we have a picture of the possibility of man and a revelation of the character of God. Aside from all petty questioning, we find certainty concerning man's relationship to

FINDING THE FUNDAMENTALS

man, man's relationship to God, and God's relationship to man. In the Bible we find the assurance that man's immortal aspirations shall be satisfied.

In the Bibles given to soldiers and sailors in the late war were inscribed the words of Woodrow Wilson, "When you have read the Bible you will know that it is the word of God because you have found it the key to your own heart, your own happiness, and your own duty."

Bishop Haygood was far ahead of his day in this discriminating statement: "Does Moses say, 'I, Moses, son of Amram and Jochebed, wrote all that is in these five books?' If so, where does he say it? Does Isaiah say, 'I, Isaiah, son of Amoz, wrote every one of these sixty-six chapters?' If so, where does he say it? It is Christianity and not a theory of inspiration nor the authorship of certain books in the Bible that we are fighting for. In what least particular would a dozen pens in the Pentateuch or twice a dozen in Isaiah affect Christianity? There in the evangelists is Jesus Christ. He is Christianity."

The universal truths are self-evidencing and form a perfect answer to the questionings of the human spirit. The principles and doctrines of Jesus bear the marks of ultimateness and universality.

It is impossible to enclose the vital gospel

within a system of cold abstract definitions. You might as well attempt to gather all the perfume of the springtime flowers into a bottle. You might as well attempt to catch all the beauty of all the landscapes in a kodak. But there are some truths that are basic and fundamental:

1. God is our Father, with the necessary postulate of human brotherhood.

2. There is the fact of Jesus Christ: His incarnation, atonement, resurrection, and ascension.

3. There is the presence and power of the Holy Spirit.

4. Man is the child of God and immortal.

5. There is the fact of the kingdom of God, spiritual and universal in its nature.

All of these mean a right relationship between man and God and between man and man.

We are to keep the central message distinct and emphatic. This is our safety and strength. Dr. W. N. Clarke makes this forceful utterance and discrimination: "We do not keep our central message distinct in its glory as we ought to do; but we bind up with it all our views of the Bible, of doctrine, and even of Church polity. All incidental and secondary matters ought to be presented as incidental and secondary, and the great elemental truths ought to be kept in their solitary glory and tenderness. Even the Bible itself is not the end of faith, but only the means to an end. The ultimate object of our faith is Jesus Christ, and God the Father whom he reveals to the world. The puzzled hearer may exclaim, 'What do we know of God except through the Bible?' Yes, and what do we know of the stars except through the telescope? And yet the telescope is not the star, and the only use of the telescope is that the star may be revealed. The Bible is the telescope and God is the star, the sun.''

Many of our human notions are at the point of vanishing and ought to vanish, but the truths of eternal value abide forever. They are forever beyond the reach of any sort of criticism, reverent or irreverent. They are deeply and eternally imbedded both in the heart of God and in the spirit of man. The precious diamond of God's revelation has often changed its setting in human thought; it may change it again, but the diamond will always sparkle with untarnished splendor. The background of our faith may change its coloring. It has changed it in the past; but the essential, vital faith in the saving love of God as manifested in Jesus Christ will remain so long as there are human need and divine compassion. These fundamentals of the Christian faith constitute our inner line of defense from which we can never be driven.

In human warfare it has often happened that an army that has retreated from some position at last found itself in an inner circle of defense that was invincible. The German assault on Verdun for two long months was the most terrific conflict in the annals of battle. Outer lines were broken through, but the main line held, the inner circle of defense was impregnable. The words of General Petain, "They shall not pass," thrilled the heart and nerved the arm of every French soldier. In the last desperate assault of the Crown Prince, 40,000 German soldiers were slaughtered in a hopeless effort to pass the French curtain of fire. The main line held.

In the conflict for the faith some outer lines of human systems and man-made creeds have been broken through; and while much ammunition has been wasted by theologians in defending indefensible positions, there is an inner citadel of the faith from which no long-range enemy guns can ever drive us. There is the unbreakable line which no terrific onslaught can ever bend.

These vital truths—God our Father, Jesus Christ our Saviour, the presence of the Holy Spirit, man an immortal child of God, and the reign of Jesus Christ, all held in the warm clasp of a living experience—are beyond the reach of all the deadly projectiles and poisonous gases of the enemies of our faith. "There is the removing of those things that are shaken as of things that are made, that those things that cannot be shaken may remain."

CHAPTER II

THE PRAGMATIC TEST OF CHRISTIAN DOCTRINE

In order to get a running start some seven other tests of the essential verities of the faith will be briefly considered before discussing the pragmatic test.

Very much is being said as to what constitutes the fundamentals. The writer lays claim to being a fundamentalist if you do not begin the word with a capital letter. There is a group who make the boast of being one hundred per cent orthodox. Another group boasts of being one hundred per cent American.

An Irishman recently landed goes them one better and says: "I'm a two hundred per cent American; I hate everybody."

The religious Pharisees can never be accused of despising themselves. They are somewhat like the old brother in Georgia who always insisted on using the wrong preposition in the lines of the familiar hymn and sang with a voice above all the others:

> "Sweet prospects, sweet birds, and sweet flowers
> Have all lost their sweetness *but* me."

With one voice we have a group among us who sing, "Have all lost their sweetness but me."

Their sweetness, however, is not very evident in the vitriolic attacks which they make on their theological opponents.

The faith is really endangered when we so link what is essential and indubitable with what is unessential and doubtful, that the two in our thoughts stand or fall together.

There is the proneness of the Church to confuse the essential and incidental matters. We have magnified the transient and passing into an equality with the permanent and abiding. The mind of the Church should be saved from confusion.

With the Christian minister, next to the obligation of saving the lost is the obligation of enlightening the saved.

I

The first test is the determinative revelation of Jesus Christ. The revelation of God in Jesus Christ must ever be the central sun of all our thought. Premillennialists who contend for what they term fundamentalism can find encouragement for the physical reign of Christ on earth for a thousand years from the teaching of Jesus only by the most strained interpretation. The same is true of their literalistic notions of

THE PRAGMATIC TEST

inspiration. Their favorite literature is the apocalyptic portions of the Scripture.

All the religious ideas of men and every part of the Bible itself must meet the test of Christ's life and teaching and character. Of all other teachers it may be said:

> "They are but broken lights of Thee,
> And Thou, O Lord, art more than they."

Bishop A. G. Haygood wrote: "Whatever in the Old Testament writings, no matter who holds the pens, is in harmony with Jesus Christ and his teaching is true. If any man should find in any of them anything that contradicts him or antagonizes his teaching, it is false. Jesus Christ is the supreme test of truth, in word, in deed, in motive, in life."

II

There is the subjective test of human experience. The essential nature of every doctrine may be tested by experience. The crowning evidence of a Christian idea is its verification in experience. All the vital truths of the Christian faith are verified in human experience. I know by experience that the Son of Man has power on earth to forgive sin, but it would be very foolish to say that I know by experience what the apostolic mode of water baptism was. I know by experience God as my Father and the

the blessedness of fellowship with him, but I cannot know by experience who wrote the books of the Bible.

> "If e'er, when faith had fallen asleep,
>   I heard a voice, 'Believe no more,'
>   And heard an ever-breaking shore
> That tumbled in the godless deep,
>
> A warmth within the breast would melt
>   The freezing reason's colder part,
>   And, like a man in wrath, the heart
> Stood up and answered, 'I have felt.'
>
> Whoso has felt the spirit of the highest
>   Cannot confuse nor doubt him nor deny,
> Yea, with our voice, 'O world, though thou deniest,
>   Stand thou on that side, for on this am I.'"

III

A further test of the essentials is the common experience of all who have access to the facts. This is both a corroboration of the experience of the individual and the correction of the abnormalities of individual subjectivity. "It is to comprehend with all the saints." L. F. Stearns writes: "Multitudes in all ages have tried the gospel method, and have found peace in believing. The new life, fellowship with the Father, and the forgiveness of sins have become realities to them. The keenest and most cultivated intellects have found satisfaction in this realm of knowledge. Multitudes have given their lives in testimony of their conviction that these sacred facts are what Christianity claims."

IV

There is the test of a historical foundation. The Christian faith rests not on the mists that arise out of the fancy of the subjective mind. The myths and marvels that gather about the cradle of the non-Christian religions are without historical evidence. The apostles of the Christian faith speak after this manner: "That which was from the beginning, which we have heard, which we have seen with our eyes, which we have looked upon, and our hands have handled, of the Word of life." St. Paul, in 1 Corinthians xv. 1-8, records the evidence of the death and resurrection of Jesus Christ, which occurred only twenty-five or twenty-six years before. The greater part of five hundred eye-witnesses of his resurrection were living. St. Paul was converted two or three years after the crucifixion of Jesus. The historical events on which the gospel is based were not hidden in a dim and remote past. Belief in the Fatherhood of God and the love of God will persist because the Son of God lived with humanity and died for humanity. Christianity is not only a spiritual but a historical religion.

V

A test of an essential religious element is that it enters into a harmonious relation with the whole body of assured knowledge. The idea of one God has finally won out over the notion of many gods, because it is in accord with the scientific knowledge of the unity of the universe. The former orthodox notion of the age of the world is out of harmony with the established facts of science and cannot survive. Various superstitions have become impossible. It is one glory of our religion rightly understood and interpreted that it can live in the modern world with the most accurate knowledge and the most searching investigation, and not come into the slightest contradiction with any proved fact of modern knowledge. The Christian faith can never go out of date or get behind the times. Romanes elaborates at some length on the timeless quality of the words of Christ. No lapse of time can ever antiquate his teachings. Many of our conceptions of religion are destined for the scrapheap, but essential Christianity can never be discredited by a growing knowledge of the universe.

VI

There is the verdict of the racial and human instinct. Religion from the beginning has been

THE PRAGMATIC TEST

an indestructible possession of the human race. There has been the belief in some sort of a God, however crude. The instinct of immortality is traced back to the glacial period. Every race or tribe has believed in a ghost world. The ethical instinct has co-existed with these other beliefs. There has been in the most ignorant savages some imperfect sense of right and wrong and the freedom of man. So you have the great doctrines of God, immortality and freedom, testified to by this old and enduring instinct of the race.

Is it possible that the instincts in the lower realm of man's personality and the instincts of the animals are true, while the instincts in the higher realm of man's personality have simply mocked man with a delusion when they have called him to an unseen spiritual universe? Is the instinct of the bird and bee true and this instinct of the human heart false?

> "I go to prove my soul.
> I see my way as birds their trackless way.
> I shall arrive; what time, what circuit first,
> I ask not; but unless God send his hail
> Or blinding fireballs, sleet, or stifling snow,
> In some time, his good time, I shall arrive;
> He guides me and the bird. In his good time."

The expression of the spiritual instincts and aspirations of mankind, while manifesting itself in varied forms, at the same time is marked by many features that are alike. Much discussion has taken place concerning the likeness of certain elements of the Christian faith to the mystery religions of Paganism. The liberal school has been disposed to use these resemblances to discredit the Christian gospel as if it had borrowed its doctrines and sacraments from paganism. Christian apologists have been too prone to ignore the points of resemblance and claim that paganism in its later forms borrowed from the Christian faith. As a general proposition neither of these suppositions is correct. Human life with the same spiritual hunger and the same aspirations, reaching out after God, though widely separated by space and time, will express its search for the divine in ways that are very much alike. That which the unbeliever uses as an objection is an argument for the Christian faith. It is not something foreign to the agelong groping of the races of men, but holds before men in the highest form that which they have been stumbling toward, but have not been able to reach in their own unaided strength and wisdom.

Jesus Christ carries the evidence of being the Son of Man and the Son of God because He gathers up in his own person all the truer instincts of the groping mind and aspiring heart of humanity through the climbing centuries. His preëminence is that He does not stand out in any startling innovation as some mistaken defenders would claim. We are not surprised that ancient sages and saints have left on record sayings that are very much like many words of Jesus.

> "Though truths in manhood darkly join,
> Deep-seated in our mystic frame,
> We yield all blessing to the name
> Of him that made them current coin."

VII

The doctrines must be true which arise in response to a real human need. For the physical need of man, there is the outside material world which responds to his need. What life begins to need, what it feels from within that it must have, is eventually supplied.

> "But fresh and green from the rotting roots
> Of primal forests the young growth shoots;
> From the death of the old, the new proceeds,
> And the life of truth from the rot of creeds;
> On the ladder of God which upward leads
> The steps of progress are human needs."

I used this argument on a friend when I was away on a vacation trip, and when he had committed himself to it I told him that I needed ten dollars. He replied that there were exceptions to all rules.

The need of the infant finds its response in the love of the mother. As the life of man expands from infancy the need is met. The growing intellect finds a world of laws and literature. The social need is met by playmates and companions. The craving for beauty is met by the sunset sky, the majestic mountains, and all the beauties of nature and art. As love is awakened, a fair face emerges from the throng, fairer to us than all the rest.

As religious want arises, it is met by personal fellowship with God. As the earthly life finishes its course, we are confident that man's conscious need of immortality will be met. The need is evidence of the God who satisfies the need. Is the spiritual need of man, his deepest, highest need for guidance and forgiveness, related to a mere illusion? Does the deepest need of man constitute the one dark exception? It is unreasonable to suppose that through the ages all life, from the lowest up to man in his physical need, has been related to an external satisfying reality, while the highest spiritual need of man in laying hold of a spiritual world has related itself to an unreality. This is to do violence to all common sense and reason. The Bible is secure for all the future both against the attack of its foes and the false defense of its friends, because it contains the revelation of the kind of God humanity needs. There is a skeptical objection to religion because it arises out of a sense of need. But what stronger argument could you have? A kind of world and order of things in which there is a response to the need of humanity is what we would expect of a God who is our Creator and Father. When we come into possession of that which satisfies our deepest need, our spiritual need, we have laid hold of "the things that cannot be shaken, the things that remain."

VIII

The final test is the pragmatic test or working value of a belief. This test of working values is illustrated in the individual character: "By their fruits ye shall know them." A faith which enables men to overcome the world and victoriously to bear the burden and heat of life's day thereby makes strong confirmation of its truthfulness. It should be plain to us that nothing is fundamental in religion that brings to us no moral motive power. The faith which produces the best type of life and character is to be regarded as true. Every doctrine which makes men bitter and contentious, which prevents the fruit of the spirit, love, joy, peace, long-suffering, kindness, goodness, faithfulness, meekness, and temperance, is by that fact proclaimed to be an imperfect or perverted conception of the truth. This method will not result in a vague, uncertain faith. It is only a clear, vital faith which will enable us to practice the principles of Jesus.

A Baptist brother told me that in a meeting of an Association he observed that the arm of an old preacher was swollen from shoulder to finger tips. He asked: "Why, brother, what is the trouble with your arm?" The old brother replied: "Well, it was this way: I went to a barbecue in the country, and coming home late in the afternoon I thought a pear would help my digestion. I went down to the orchard as it was getting dark and reached up for a pear and it was a hornet's nest."

The old brother's belief was not workable and came very near costing him his life. We cannot say with our Christian Science friends, that it was the result of an error of the mortal mind, since if the hornet's nest had been empty there would have been the same error of the mortal mind, but the arm would not have been swollen. We are not to underestimate the value of a true faith.

The test of workability is illustrated in the whole sphere of public life. In a world which God has made we may expect the essential truths to stand the test of workability. Christlieb, a noted philosopher, said: "In a world created by a God who is good, that which introduces disorder and confusion is convicted of being false." So the question is raised, What is

THE PRAGMATIC TEST

the practical value of a belief which claims to be true? Does it work well in life and lead to satisfactory results? The truth is the only practical thing in the world. I make no claim to any extensive knowledge of Pragmatism as a philosophy, but I accept without reserve the practical test.

In a world which the devil made, evil and error would fit in and would be natural for that kind of a world. Purity, truthfulness, faith, and love in the devil's world would be against nature.

The absurd contradiction is that while we live in a world which God made, yet the laws of the devil are the only practical laws, and the laws of God are only a form of poetical language. There is a Supreme Ruler, but his laws and truths will not work in his world. "Thou shalt love thy neighbor as thyself" is visionary, and the Golden Rule is a figure of speech. The Sermon on the Mount is an iridescent dream. The Ten Commandments are not for the rough and tumble of everyday life. "It is more blessed to give than to receive" is a beautiful sentiment, but is not intended for practice. So men have tried to run God's world with the devil's laws.

What have been the results in the social and economic world of assuming that greed and selfishness are the only workable rules? In such a world dissatisfaction and disorder are a necessity. With a million or a thousand million wills working for their own selfish desires nothing but unrest and conflict are possible. The gulf which separates the employed from the employing classes is so deep and wide that it appears almost impossible to bridge the chasm. Unless unselfishness shall take the place of greed and cutthroat competition, the world's last and greatest war will be that of capital and labor. Is it not about time to inquire as to whether the laws of the devil are really practical laws, whether the maxim, "Every man for himself and the devil take the hindermost," is going to work well in our world?

Frederick Robertson is far enough removed from us in time to add force to his prophetic words: "Brethren, that which is built on selfishness cannot stand. The system of personal self-interest must be shivered into atoms. Therefore, we who have observed the ways of God in the past are waiting in quiet but awful expectation until he shall confound this system as he has confounded those which have gone before. And it may be effected by convulsions more terrible and more bloody than the world has yet seen. While men are talking of peace and the great progress of civilization there is heard in the distance the noise of armies gathering rank upon rank, east and west, north and south, and rolling toward us the crashing thunders of universal war."

Take, for example, impurity. The law of purity and holiness is esteemed too high for human realization. Novelists glorify vice and unchastity. Imagination transfigures it and places a glamour about it.

There belongs to it the fascinating allurement and almost irresistible power that comes from the blending of passion and mystery. There is to-day the revel of sensuality. But the artificial fascination is removed when the rose is stricken from the cheeks of beauty and the blister of shame takes its place. The triangular affair becomes a red triangle at the sharp crack of a pistol. As impurity works in society the law courts are filled with divorce suits, innocent children are subjected to the unspeakable pathos of alienated parents, and if generally practiced it would mean the destruction of the home and the wreck of civilization. One out of every seven marriages in the United States ends in a divorce court. In 1870 we had twenty-eight divorces for every one hundred thousand of the population; in 1922 the figures increased to one hundred and thirty-four for every one hundred thousand. A large number of these divorces are the result of marital infidelity. If you would know how impurity is working, you must reckon with the heavy toll of disease and suffering and the destruction of home life.

How does the spirit of revenge work? It is

not a workable rule between individuals. As it widens the circle, it would transform society into a cage of wild beasts. Europe waded through seas of blood, destroying millions of of lives and billions of property, to discover that not the strife of nations, but the brotherhood of nations is the only workable principle. Men have been obsessed by military pomp, and the ladies have been obsessed by uniforms and brass buttons. The whole wretched business is insane and criminal.

Again dishonesty and trickery have been considered necessary in business. A recent book by Babson, a leading expert in business, is extensively quoted because he has convincingly contended that religion is necessary to prosperity. The editor of the *Wall Street Journal,* who would hardly be accused of being a sentimentalist, said that the man who believes in God is a better man to transact business with than one who has no such faith.

Does intemperance work well in the world? It was at first supposed that the objectors were visionary reformers. The final staggering blow is given to intemperance as it is shown to be unworkable even from the viewpoint of this world. Mr. Edison says: "Society will have to stop the liquor business, which is like throwing sand into the bearings of an engine." It is in essence

THE PRAGMATIC TEST

a religious question throughout simply because intemperance will not work in God's world.

There are those who hold that race prejudice and the denial of brotherhood are the workable rules in society. But the men who arouse racial enmity, even though it may be done under the false plea of religion or patriotism, are the enemies of order in our world. The one hopeful outlook for the future is that Christianity will succeed in curing racial enmities.

An Anglo-Saxon snobbishness that irritates and antagonizes the vast population of the colored races of the world carries with it the possibility of the very destruction of our civilization.

There is nothing practical in the world except Christian truth. Mankind has tried everything except Christianity. The world has tried hatred, greed, revenge, impurity, graft, self-interest, and has been brought to the brink of perdition. It is curious that we must stand up in the twentieth century and plead with the people who bear his name that Jesus Christ is not a foolish ruler, a visionary leader, that his word is the illuminating word, that his way is the living way, that it is only safe to trust and follow him. The Church must repent of her lukewarmness and rebuke with prophetic wrath the selfishness of men and break her cowardly silence and say to the world, we have let you run affairs after your selfish pagan methods until you have come to the brink of ruin; unless you Christianize your industrial system, it cannot last; unless you Christionize your institutions, they cannot endure. "Other foundation can no man lay than that is laid, which is Jesus Christ." Too long have we imagined that the principles of Christ were for some other world. We have put the kingdom he came to establish beyond the stars. But this was not the purpose of his mission, this is not the meaning of his gospel. His laws are to be followed in the world in which we live, now and here, in street and market and factory. If you fail to live his laws here, you will have no chance to live them in heaven. It will only be through obedience to the moral law, and the Sermon on the Mount, and the Golden Rule, and a whole-hearted response to the Fatherhood of God and brotherhood of man and the suffering love of Jesus Christ that there can ever be a frictionless society in our world. When we say that Christ is our only hope, we have been accustomed to suppose that he is our only hope merely for the future world. But we are beginning to see, as we have not seen before, that Christ is our only hope in this world. He alone can save us from a hell in this present world. If in the future life only we have hope in Christ, we are of all men most miserable.

The fundamental faith is the faith which best

satisfies the soul's need and works best in life. If our religion is able to cast out the devils of pride, selfishness, greed, hate, and revenge, it can ignore the cheap flings of skepticism. If it cannot do that, it is useless to fall back on abstract theories of apologetics.

It is not short of absurdity that men should endeavor to frame their apologetics for the Christian faith on whether some ancient and obscure prophecy is literally fulfilled, whereas the fact that the only workable ideal is the Christian ideal is an overwhelming evidence for the Christian faith which is as fresh as the dew of the morning and as clear as the sunlight. The Christian faith is true because it is the only faith that fits our world, the only faith that is adapted to the complex relationships of modern society, the only faith that can produce harmony and order and peace. Mr. Sherwood Eddy gives the testimony of some Chinese statesmen. A leading patriot in China says: "We need Jesus Christ to-day because we need more light. Christ comes and teaches us to think in terms of God and humanity. This is the only hope so far as I can see."

Mr. Wang, a Chinese official, testified before an immense audience: "I had hoped that the Revolution and the Republic would save China and solve her problems, but conditions only grow worse. Christianity is the only hope of saving the country." Mr. Wen, a high official, said: "I take my stand for Jesus Christ, believing that only by organized Christianity, only by the Church of Christ, can we save China."

This appeal is repeated in every part of our hopeless and restless world. When the non-Christian nations ask for bread, shall we give them the superstition of a crass Adventism? Premillennialism promotes pessimism, paralyzes patriotism, denies the hope of democracy, scoffs at social progress, scorns all sane ideals of Christianizing the world, with its superficial idea of heralding the gospel as the mere condition of setting up a physical kingdom of Christ. You cannot reasonably suppose for a moment that the premillennial program can make any appeal to the thoughtful and intelligent among the heathen nations, a program summed up in the classic of the cult, "Jesus is coming." Premillennialism is the greatest religious hindrance to genuine missionary service. It has no faith in the workability of the gospel in society. According to its crude conception, nothing will work but a celestial militarism, in which Jesus Christ will exercise more than the might and cruelty of a Kaiser. These advocates of crude adventism have no confidence in the improvement of the present world order; they are the hopeless followers of a Gospel of Hope.

Whatever may be the explanation of Biblical

interpreters concerning some apocalyptic elements in the teaching of Jesus, we know that the very heart and life of his revelation is both a right relationship of man to God and a harmonious relationship of men with men.

Professor Ellwood has forcefully written: "The social principles of Jesus are so plainly the only ones by which men can live satisfactorily together that they might just as well forget the law of gravitation as to forget these principles. When one forgets the principles of gravitation, one must expect some hard bumps; so when our human world forgets these principles of right living together, it must expect some hard lessons —such as it has been receiving. . . . A Christian world is not only practicable; in the long run it will be found that no other sort is **practicable.**"

Whatever defects may belong to the pragmatic philosophy, the pragmatic test is valuable and justifiable. "By their fruits ye shall know them." That which works continuously for good must be in harmony with the nature of man and of the world in which he is placed, and that which works for evil carries the evidence of its falseness.

The ultimate test of anything is that we have tried it and it works.

Let us imagine that, beginning with to-morrow, the spirit and truth of Jesus Christ should dominate all men. According to Lecky, the historian, "the simple record of these short years of Christ's active life has done more to regenerate and soften mankind than all the disquisitions of philosophers and all the exhortations of moralists."

Suppose every man lived in the faith of divine Fatherhood and human brotherhood and eternal life and eternal love.

Suppose that the Christian ideas of liberty, justice, brotherhood, and peace prevailed in human society.

Suppose that the Christian spirit of unselfishness and sacrifice were dominant in human life.

Then all the economic and political conditions of the world would be immensely improved, the selfish conflict of capital and labor would cease, war would be relegated to the barbarism of the past.

There would be no evil lust or avarice, no drunkenness. The earth would become a house fit for the children of God to live in.

These ideals which, incarnate in life and applied to life, would change earth into heaven cannot be false.

On the other hand, whatever is against the Christian faith or falls short of the Christian faith is condemned because it does not fit in with the world order.

Professor Hocking, of Harvard, says: "If a

THE PRAGMATIC TEST 51

theory has no consequences, or bad ones; if it makes no difference to men, or undesirable differences;' if it lowers the capacity of men to meet the stress of existence, or diminishes the worth to them of what existence they have, such a theory is somehow false, and we have no peace until it is remedied."

The last word against the non-Christian faith is that it is not practical in our everyday working world.

Polygamy was finally condemned, not from any theoretical or speculative standpoint, but because it produced endless confusion and disorder in society and obstructed the progress of civilization.

The institution of slavery was at last overthrown, not by invincible arguments that demonstrated it to be against the will of God, but because in its practical application it was shown to be unwise even from an economic standpoint.

The final logic that is prevailing against intemperance is the logic of life.

The religious argument of preachers and prohibition reformers, while laying the foundation of ultimate victory, was considered visionary by the mass of men. But when the people were at last awakened to the fact that intemperance was bad business, then its final death knell was sounded.

Professor Rauschenbusch gives this neat turn

to an urgent question: "Is Christianity a failure? I deny it. The question is in order whether anything in the history of humanity has succeeded except Christianity."

The Christian faith is the timeless and final religion since it has the developing capacity and the eternal message which enables it to meet the needs of any age and of all ages.

Not only the power in heaven, but the power on earth belongs to Jesus Christ, a power that is inherent in the very structure and laws of our world, which are the allies of the forces of righteousness.

> "For right is right, since God is God,
> And right the day must win;
> To doubt would mean disloyalty,
> To falter would be sin."

CHAPTER III

THE FALLACY OF THE FALSE ALTERNATIVE

THE fallacy of the false alternative is one of the most fatal of all forms of loose logic.

Anaxagoras said twenty-five hundred years ago that men are always cutting the world in two with a hatchet. William James in his own unique way said that everybody dichotomizes the cosmos. Such simple words are crystal clear. There is a true statement of alternatives when one is true and the other false. We may choose the true. There is the false statement of alternatives when both alternatives are false and we are called upon to choose between them, or when both alternatives are true and we are called upon to choose between them.

F. W. Boreham, essayist, writes: "Which will you have, strawberries or cream? I will take both strawberries and cream. We are too fond of taking the strawberries from the cream and the cream from the strawberries. I have on my plate here not two things but one thing, and that one thing is strawberries and cream. Dissection is not in my line. I only know that I thoroughly enjoy strawberries and cream."

Had you rather be a happy pig or an unhappy philosopher? You don't have to be either. You can be a happy philosopher.

Some false alternatives in general will be named before proceeding to those with their direct social bearing.

I

We are called upon to choose between faith and reason. But faith is not believing the absurd; it is believing the reasonable. Christianity makes its appeal to the reasonable and has no place for credulity and superstition.

II

We are called upon to choose between faith and good works. A defender of the first says, "The pendulum of good works has swung us too far from God." Must we choose then between believing the gospel and living the gospel? Why not have both?

III

There is the false alternative, God or Law.
This sets nature and God over against each other. As men came to recognize the reign of

THE FALSE ALTERNATIVE

law, God was relegated to the gaps and exceptions, and these were constantly being narrowed down. God dwelt in chaos instead of in the cosmos. So the theories of Copernicus and Newton were all considered at first anti-religious. The ancients knew little of natural law, and all the various phenomena of nature were attributed to various gods.

The fallacy obtained that wherever natural law is seen a personal will is excluded.

Browning writes:

> "I report the world as I saw it;
> All is Love, yet all is Law."

There has prevailed the error of seeing God only in chaos and in the realm of the lawless. God was seen only in the phenomena for which no natural explanation had been found. The discovery of the law of gravitation was resisted as leading to atheism. We are now understanding that the reign of law enhances the glory of God, that laws are God's method of working and that he is the infinite and eternal energy from which all things proceed. The false antithesis is removed.

Lord Kelvin, one of the world's great scientists, said: "If you think strongly enough, you will be forced by science to the belief in God. You will find science not antagonistic, but helpful, in religion."

IV

In recent months much emphasis has been placed on the antithesis, belief in evolution or being a Christian.

I am not a scientific expert; but, aside from all discussion of scientific hypotheses, we must reject this as a false alternative.

Leading Fundamentalists are constantly picturing the sad ending, the moral and spiritual collapse that has overtaken evolutionists and historical critics. I do not pose as a scientific expert on scientific questions, but I claim discernment enough to see that this method of argument gets nowhere.

A large company of Biblical scholars like Marcus Dods and George Adam Smith have held to a vital Christian faith in the fundamental verities that has lifted their moral life above reproach. The well-worn illustration of the atrophy of the spiritual faculties of Darwin through a one-sided and absorbing devotion to science is constantly narrated. There is the convenient omission, however, of Romanes, who was driven to God in his old age by the discovery of the Divine Spirit in the processes of Nature. No mention is made of John Fiske, who was brought by his study of evolution to believe in God. In his closing chapter on "Through Nature to God"

THE FALSE ALTERNATIVE 57

he writes: "Of all the implications of the doctrine of evolution with regard to man, I believe the very deepest and strongest to be that which asserts the everlasting reality of religion."

The theorizing of the Fundamentalists is against the facts. When a theory contradicts a fact, something will be broken, and it will not be the fact. There is the old story of the lawyer who said to his client: "Why, they can't put you in jail." The reply of the client was: "Yes, but I'm in jail."

Against the censorious claims that men cannot hold certain views and at the same time be Christians is the indisputable fact of Christian life and character. Henry Drummond wrote "The Ascent of Man." It is aside from my subject to pronounce on the correctness of his evolutionary hypothesis. My sole aim is to refute the old *ad hominem* argument that so many controversialists are at present repeating. In George Adam Smith's masterful biography of Henry Drummond we have an almost ideal picture of an almost ideal spirit. D. L. Moody and Drummond were as far apart as the poles in some of their views, but the young scientist gave himself to Christ under the preaching of Moody in 1871 and became his devoted friend and faithful coworker. Mr. Moody says: "No word of mine can better describe his character than do those which he presents to us in 'The Greatest

Thing in the World!' Some men take an occasional journey into the thirteenth chapter of First Corinthians, but Henry Drummond was a man who lived in it. As you read what he terms the analysis of love, you find that all of its ingredients were interwoven into his daily life, making him one of the most lovable men I have ever known. Was it courtesy you looked for, he was a perfect gentleman; was it kindness, he was always preferring another; was it humility, he was simple and not courting favor. It could be said of him truthfully, as it was said of the early apostles, 'that men took knowledge of him, that he had been with Jesus.' Nor was this love and kindness only shown to those who were his close friends. His face was an index to his inner life. It was genial and kind and made him, like his Master, a favorite with children. Never have I known a man who, in my opinion, lived nearer the Master, or sought to do his will more fully. No man has ever been with me for any length of time that I did not see something that was unlike Christ, and I often see it in myself, but not in Henry Drummond. All the time we were together he was a Christlike man, and often a rebuke to me. He always made me conscious of my sinfulness. Dr. John Watson said: 'He is the most perfect man I ever knew.'"

George Adam Smith wrote: "I have never seen in any man so much that was admirable,

THE FALSE ALTERNATIVE

for he seemed to possess all the graces and virtues of a perfect man." One night he returned from evangelistic services in Edinburgh and was found with his face in his hands. In reply to a question, he answered with a groan: "Sick with the sins of men. How can God bear it?" But with this Christlike compassion, in the opinion of some modern traditionalists, Drummond was not a Christian because of his scientific beliefs. Mr. Moody, although a conservative in theology, offers a refreshing contrast to this type of bigotry. When an effort was made to persuade him not to allow Drummond to speak at Northfield, he replied that Drummond was a better man than himself, and so would be allowed to speak. Drummond remarked to an attendant physician a month before his death: "Moody is the biggest human I ever met."

Henry Drummond believed with all his heart that this is God's world, and that a fact is a fact and a very stubborn thing wherever found, and that the facts of science and religion can never be in contradiction to each other. He said to Gladstone and Huxley, who were in controversy: "You are both wrong, especially in what you agree on; the Christian revelation does not depend on the reconciliation of Genesis and geology. Your whole discussion is as irrelevant as the question of the Senior Wrangler who asked what Milton's 'Paradise

Lost' was intended to prove." Drummond claimed that the first principle and the ruling principle in the interpretation of any book is the dominant purpose or motive of the whole. The dominant purpose in the case of the Bible reduces itself to one thing, religion. To have revealed to men modern science in the childhood of the race would not only have been an anachronism, but a source of mystification and confusion. He confidently believed that in the realm of religion the Bible has brought to us a revelation which man could never have originated, and which man can never supersede. He bore with perfect temper all the vicious attacks that were made, and remarked: "It is hard to be called names, but the disciple is not above his Master." When sorrow came, he said: "How suddenly the water deepens, sometimes, in one's life. Well, I suppose it must be better, this deeper sea, than the shallows where the children play."

Would not Mr. Drummond compare fairly well at least with the best of the Fundmentalists as a genuine Christian?

V

We have been made familiar with the false alternative, the Bible is either the Word of God or the work of man.

THE FALSE ALTERNATIVE 61

It never occurs to certain controversialists with a bisecting mania that the Bible represents both the Word of God and the work of man.

VI

There is the common false alternative of conservatism or progress. Why not have both? Why not conserve the good and let it pass into the better and the best? We should not be swerved aside from the truth either by rigid conservatism or reckless radicalism.

Jesus tells us that the wise householder brings forth out of his treasure, not things new or old, but things new and old.

How we fuss over words and try to impale each other on the horns of a false dilemma.

VII

The false distinction of sacred or secular was introduced by the Roman Catholic Church. The ministry is sacred, while business is secular. A selfish policy is thus permitted to trade and industry, but not to preaching the gospel. Dr. Josiah Strong wrote: "Yes, there are two worlds in conflict, whose struggle is as old as man, but they are not the sacred and secular; the so-called secular is a fiction. It is not the material and spiritual worlds; they were made to supplement one another that they might both serve God. The struggle is between the world of selfishness and the world of love, one of which is necessarily individualistic, while the other is social."

VIII

There is the false alternative of interest in time or eternity. Our regard must be for both. An otherworldliness which draws motive power from the heavenly world makes us strong for the duties of the present world. In a slightly different form the "either or" fallacy is interest in the world and its future welfare or interest in our own future in the heavenly world. We should choose both. We may not live long in this world, but other people may be here for a long stretch of time.

IX

There is the false alternative of soul or body. Jesus in his preaching and healing placed honor on both. Holiness and health are from the same root word. The body and soul are very close neighbors and each one catches the ailments of the other.

X

We are faced with the false alternative of regeneration or eugenics. There is a notion that good ancestry solves everything. A frequent

THE FALSE ALTERNATIVE 63

trouble with dead ancestors is that they are not dead enough. But while we see the failure of mere ancestry, we likewise see the force of it. The preacher who ridicules eugenics, or being well born, carefully considers it when it comes to the marriage of his own children. The preacher is standing on a sound scriptural foundation when he denounces the licentiousness of the young man and the mercenary marriage of the young woman, because "the iniquities of the fathers are visited upon the children."

We do well to stress both regeneration and eugenics. A person who is well born the first time stands a better chance for the new and second birth. The alternative is as false as that created by the boy with his little brother. "Did you give your little brother the choice of the apples as I told you?" "Yes, mama, I told him that he could take the little one or none and he took the little one."

XI

We are called upon to make a choice between the power of the gospel and environment. Extreme advocates of environment deny the reality of sin. In a long struggle with hostile, vicious surroundings, selfish tendencies are developed. They tell us that if we make environments wholesome and people are well fed and well clothed the angelic qualities of human nature readily appear. But our first parents and the fallen angels were in good surroundings. But why deny the power of environment?

There are surroundings of poverty, filth, and vice in which people hardly have a fighting chance. Multiplied thousands are hardened by the cruel competition of modern industry. They care no more for sin and redemption and immortal life than for a last year's almanac. In the face of a situation like this the other type of extremist by way of ridiculing environment raises the alternative, salvation or sunshine, salvation or soup, salvation or soap. We don't have to make the choice; we can have all of them. We have friends whom we would dislike very much to see discard the use of soap. This species of alliterative alternative becomes wearisome and monotonous. A hearty recognition of the value of human agencies while at the same time confessing their insufficiency is most conducive to a sane viewpoint. We have observed that the men who ridicule the power of environment are anxious that their children shall live in good surroundings.

You recognize the advantage of children being brought up under the influence of the Church and Sunday school. The fight against the whisky saloon was a fight for better surroundings. We wish to discourage some brethren from encouraging the extreme which they ridicule. When

THE FALSE ALTERNATIVE

you minimize certain forces and agencies in the individual and social life which men know to be true, you weaken your argument for the direct, divine agency which is forever true. Do not feed fuel to the foolish extreme which you wish to ridicule. Beware of the "either or" fallacy. Why raise the issue of a choice between the gospel and a good environment? Of two good things, choose both.

A preacher friend with whom I dined asked if the good wife should help me to fried chicken or chicken pie. I did not wish to appear exorbitant in my request, but I was compelled to reply that I could not choose between the two, and that I would take both. Do not ask if we will take coffee or sugar. Please give us coffee and sugar.

XII

There is the false alternative, service for God or service for humanity.

An ecclesiastic is quoted in the *Homiletic Review* as saying: "There are those who assume to correct the Church and undertake to constrain her to renounce her position, contract her mission, and exchange the service of God for the service of humanity. They would have her abandon her high calling in Jesus Christ and give herself up to programs of social betterment." The Church must certainly resist these extremists. But must we understand that service of God is inconsistent with the service of humanity?

Jesus called the service of "one of the least of these my little ones" as service given to him. If the Church would improve the conditions of life in the crowded and pestilential slums, must she therefore abandon her high calling? We do not have to choose between philanthropy and religion.

The partial gospel of yesterday which omitted the social note of Christ and the partial gospel of to-day which has no place for his spiritual message are alike doomed. This particular fallacy has so many forms that we rest here and carry over.

XIII

There is the choice set forth of laying stress on the individual or society, the one man or the mass of men.

Tertullian wrote in the third century, "Nothing is so foreign to Christians as public affairs." Some years ago a leading New York preacher held aloof from a moral struggle, the issue of which vitally concerned the character of the city. When it was over and the forces of righteousness and decency had been defeated he said: "I had nothing to do with it. It is my business to build character." Why should

THE FALSE ALTERNATIVE 67

any preacher think that he is called upon to choose between service to society and spiritual ministry to the individual?

A well-known writer on social questions says: "A social aim on the part of the Church does not imply neglect of the individual members of society, but rather a more efficient and intelligent care of them. Physicians no longer aim simply at curing individuals. How much larger and wiser their present purpose, which undertakes to protect society as a whole by preventive measures. Hygiene, sanitation, vaccination, and quarantine can do more to prevent sickness than all practitioners combined can do to cure it. Physicians are no less faithful in treating individuals on account of having the larger social aims. Why should not the clerical profession gain the larger conception and nobler aim as well as the medical profession?

"Moral diseases are as contagious as physical; and for a minister to refuse to help clear out gambling halls and houses of prostitution on the ground that it was his business to build character would be like a physician saying, 'It is my business to build health; I have no concern about draining swamps, killing mosquitoes, and cleaning up pest holes'—only no physician can be found ignorant enough to say such a thing."

No "either or" is permissible. Let us think both in terms of the individual and society.

XIV

There is the false alternative of salvation or legislation.

A prominent government official said: "I hope soon all Church organizations will make it their exclusive business to preach the gospel of Jesus Christ, and to reach the conclusion that the world is to be regenerated by regenerated men and women and not by regenerated laws and ordinances."

What is the objection to having both regenerated men and regenerated laws? Do not unregenerate laws indicate the character of the men who made them?

In problems of capital and labor one group advocates the "simple gospel" and says: "Get people converted and the rest will take care of itself."

The other group says: "Spend all your time changing the economic system." Both are wrong. Representatives of Wall Street take their place among the prophets and are eagerly quoted by religious journals as they piously exhort the Church to stick to the simple gospel of the conversion of the individual. One serious difficulty is that these gentlemen will not allow the Church to begin on them.

In the prohibition issue the advocacy of the

THE FALSE ALTERNATIVE

"simple gospel" carried to the logical conclusion says: "No laws; wait until the greedy saloon keeper and his rum-soaked victims are converted." Dr. W. N. Clark, with his accustomed clearness, says: "Much cynical nonsense has been talked about the impossibility of making people moral by legislation. Of course it is true that the Christian ideal of inward righteousness cannot be attained in that manner. But that is no reason why that which is possible should not be done. We cannot make men righteous by law, but by law we can make them quit a host of unrighteous practices. Society legislating can restrain the wicked and protect the weak and give life its opportunity; it can lift the pressure of injustice from many who suffer wrong; it can organize many a work of helpfulness and assist the Christian spirit in its service. The Christian ideal summons all governments to be its agents, doing what lies in their power to help it win its victory."

The individualist creates a false antithesis when he calls upon us to choose between the gospel and politics. Prohibition, child labor, and other questions having to do with social and industrial relationships are both religious and political questions.

I am a strong advocate of the old-time religion, if only you will make it old enough.

"Give me the old-time religion. It was good enough for Moses and it's good enough for me."

But Moses was the deliverer of an enslaved and oppressed people and threw out the challenge to the oppressor: "Let my people go."

The old-time religion was good enough for Isaiah, but Isaiah was sawn asunder for political meddling. The old-time religion was good enough for Amos; but Amos, with a heart aflame with indignation against injustice, rebuked with red-hot words the strong who oppressed the weak. The old-time religion was good enough for Hosea, but Hosea sobbed out of a broken heart over the social corruption of his people. In the prophetic message of Micah, George Adam Smith says: "Pinched peasant faces peer between all his words and fill the ellipses."

The old-time religion was good enough for Jesus whose express mission was "to set at liberty them that are bruised."

Those who are fond of ringing the changes on "the simple gospel" and "old-time religion" usually identify these well-worn expressions with the theological interpretation of individualism which still hinders the progress of the life and thought of the Church, and which places stress on the perpendicular relationship of life alone with a certain emotional ecstasy, and which ignores the horizontal relationships of society.

THE FALSE ALTERNATIVE

You may ask a certain type of big business man: "How many hours do your employees work?" And he replies: "Give me the old-time religion." "How much do you pay?" The response is: "I believe in the simple gospel." "What about child labor?" And again he answers: "I believe in the old-time religion."

Such men plainly hold to a perversion and parody of the good old-time religion.

There is the type of religion which concerns itself only with the salvation that is in the far future. The argument is that, while your circumstances may be all awry in this present world, you may suffer injustice, the good things of life may be most inequitably distributed, but all this is due to the inscrutable providence of God; do not meddle with the problem, it will all come right in another world. If you cannot have a piano on earth, you can have a harp in heaven. Endure for a while with pious resignation. The discipline is good for your soul here, and you will get justice and your reward beyond. Time is so short and eternity so long that you should bear any injustice without resistance.

But these bromidic solutions have failed to satisfy. Justice can no longer be postponed to another world. The demand is for justice here and now. The suffering from injustice and inhumanity must no longer be construed as the divine chastening for the disciplining of the soul. The promise of heaven is not to be used as an opiate to deaden the pain that ought not to be. The gospel was never intended as a "dope" to quiet the pangs of pain, when the cause should be removed. Salvation is not salvation merely into heaven. It is present. It is moral and ethical. It is to be interpreted in terms of justice, mercy, and love. It is to make a better social order. We have no kind of moral right to be resigned to the social wrongs and oppressions of the weak. It is a false interpretation of life and blasphemy against God to say that it is his will. We are to wage a truceless warfare against injustice and inhumanity, which are the prolific sources of so much of the woe of the world.

There are high-ups who are very much concerned that the low-downs get religion with the hope that the low-downs will be more contented with their lot. Capitalists of the individualistic sort recommend religion as an anodyne.

Religion and revivals of religion were never intended for resignation results.

The snake with a frog in its mouth is a natural optimist, but we can very easily understand why the frog is a pessimist.

There is more downright falsehood and ignorance in the fallacy of the false alternative than in any other form of logical or illogical sophistry.

I am glad of the opportunity of exposing the

THE FALSE ALTERNATIVE 73

fallacy as making some reparation for having gotten by the text-book on Logic in the course of study.

How we impoverish life with an "either or" method!

Dr. Rufus M. Jones writes these pertinent words: "Imagine a doctor bending over a patient with heart disease and saying to him, 'Never mind your heart. The all-important thing is breathing. So long as you can breathe you will live, for life consists in inhaling and exhaling air.' And then imagine another doctor of the opposite school saying to the consumptive patient, 'Never mind your lungs. Simply take good care of your heart, for life is a matter of heartbeats. So long as you can keep the blood going through the valves out into the arteries and back through the veins, you will live.' But life is not a thing that can be reduced to either heart or lungs—it must have both or it ceases to go. St. Paul found his Corinthian brethren bisecting their spiritual lives and narrowing their interests to one of two possibilities. One of them would choose Paul as his representative of faith, and see no value in the interpretation which Apollos had to give. Another attached himself to Apollos and missed all the rich contribution of Paul. Some of the saints of the Church selected Cephas as the only oracle, and they lost all breadth which would have come to them had they been able to make a synthesis of the different phases of the truth. St. Paul calls them from their divided half to a completed whole."

A question for those who have a mania for bisecting is, "Which wing does a bird fly with?"

CHAPTER IV

THE GOLDEN RULE

The very familiarity of the Golden Rule has dulled our minds to its meaning and to its variety of implications and applications. Since people in the main are not very apt in memorizing and quoting Scripture, an abbreviated form is commonly used: "Do as you would be done by."

I

There are different versions of the Golden Rule.

There are the selfish perversions, "Do the other fellow before he gets a chance to do you," and "Do unto others as they do unto you, but do it first."

There are the statements that belong to an imperfect religious conception. Rabbi Hillel said: "Do not to thy neighbor what is hateful to thyself."

Confucius said: "Do not unto others what you would not have them do unto you."

These statements are good as far as they go.

There is the philosophical expression of the Golden Rule.

Kant gives the categorical imperative: "So live that the principle of your life may be worthy of being made a universal law." This is at least a fine interpretation of the Golden Rule.

If all the people in your community had as much concern for the higher interests of the community as you, would it be a better community? If all the people should give as much to philanthropic and missionary purposes in proportion to their ability as we do, would these great enterprises be advanced?

If all the members of your Church were as devoted to the Church as we are, what would be the condition of our Church?

If all the members of the Church cared as much for the lost as we do, would there be more sinners saved by the power of the gospel?

If all who deal with their fellowmen in trade should be as anxious that the other man gets his rights as we are, would there be more harmonious relationships in society?

If all the white people should treat the negroes as we do, would the weaker race have a worse or better chance?

If other people lived by the Golden Rule as strictly as we do, would human brotherhood be promoted?

Could Jesus Christ take you as a good example for others to follow?

"So live that the principle of your life may be worthy of being made a universal law."

Let us indulge in an old form of expression that gets the ideal fully within our understanding. If everybody in the home were just like me, what kind of a home would our home be?

If everybody in the Church were just like me, what kind of a Church would our Church be?

If everybody in our community were just like me, what kind of a community would our community be?

If everybody in the nation were just like me, what kind of a nation would our nation be?

If everybody in the world were just like me, what kind of a world would our world be?

Kant again makes a suggestive interpretation of the Golden Rule: "So act as to treat humanity, whether in your own person or that of another, in every case as an end, never as a means only."

Men are prone to use their fellow men as tools for their own comfort, advancement, or pleasure.

Men of wealth, social rank, or public office frequently use their position in ignoring the personality of others, disregarding their rights, in closing against them the opportunity of development, and in other ways treating them as machines or slaves.

The true values of life are inverted and men use men to make money, instead of using money to make men.

This condition of present-day society is unchristian and wicked.

It is to be counteracted and transformed by the power of the gospel.

Each man is to respect the individuality and observe the rights of every other man.

You are to honor and treat other men as you in their places would wish to be honored and treated.

You are to give such sympathy and service to others as you would wish to receive.

In this manner the Golden Rule will take the place of the rule of gold.

"So act as to treat humanity, whether in your own person or that of another, in every case as an end, never as a means only."

II

The Golden Rule is positive.

It includes the negative aspect, yet takes a wideness of range that goes far beyond mere negative considerations. In contrast with the mere negative form you are commanded not only to avoid injuring your neighbor, but to do him all the good you can.

It stands for justice and brotherhood and

mercy and generosity. Jesus wishes by means of it to take away the mood of selfishness and contempt, which obstructs the realization of a true human brotherhood.

Negatively, it forbids my conducting myself or my affairs in such a way as to bring injury or unhappiness or ruin to other people. Positively, it commands me to treat with courtesy and consideration and conscience and compassion, superiors, equals, and inferiors as, all alike, immortal beings.

Positively, it stands for unlimited good to others, and for unlimited growth to our own spirits.

It opens up before life boundless vistas, and makes radiant every step of the ladder the whole long length of the shining way until its top rests on the threshold of the gates of pearl.

"Therefore, all things whatsoever ye would that men should do to you, do ye even so to them; for this is the law and the prophets."

III

There is the reflex influence of conforming to the Golden Rule.

It leads us to study ourselves and our real need, and then makes its inference from our need to the need of another. It makes us brotherly. It turns us from the past, what men have done to us, and turns us to the present and future, what we should do for others. It requires that our deepest and best nature shall be the guide of conduct.

With all the direct and positive good that the observance of the Golden Rule brings to other people the one unvarying good is the lifted horizon and the enlarged sympathies of your own life.

Jesus concludes his statement with, "This is the law and the prophets." In the Golden Rule the whole law of God is fulfilled. It fulfills all the prophetic visions of all the prophets of God who caught broken glimpses of the better day that is to be. It holds to a continuity with the past, and holds the promise of the future. It is as ancient as the heart of God and as new as the needs of our new day.

IV

There is a common misunderstanding of what a compliance with the Golden Rule might involve. There is the false notion that we might be placed under obligation to conform to some wish, without regard to the character of the person who makes the wish.

The arrested criminal might say truthfully to the policeman, "If you were in my place and I were in your place, I would turn you loose."

THE GOLDEN RULE

But what the unchristian spirit would have men do to them is a false standard.

The Golden Rule must have its basis in a right life, a Christlike spirit.

It can only be kept in all of its high requirements by those who know something of the transforming power of Christ in their own lives.

It is no easy precept of mere human morality.

There must be the enlightened conscience which knows how to make moral discernment and discrimination.

It is necessary that there should dwell within our hearts a Christian love, which affords the only sufficient motive power for practicing this divine principle.

There must be a high estimate of your own self. This is stated as a necessary condition: "Whatsoever ye would that men should do unto you."

You would wish that men would impart to you that which is for your own highest good. Then you are to impart to men that which is for their own highest good.

A proper appreciation of yourself and a true regard for yourself will lead you so to enrich your own life as to have something worth imparting to others. You must possess values for the other life.

There must be the cultivation of a spiritual imagination. Men have thought little of the important place of imagination as related to Christian living and the practice of the Golden Rule.

A large measure of the cruelty and oppression of earth results from the stupid incapacity of men to put themselves in the other man's place. While some artists and geniuses highly gifted in imagination have been immoral, yet very much wickedness is traceable to simple stupidity.

The imagination is the great feeder of our sympathies.

Brierly says: "The cool complacency of the well-to-do who nurse their own comfortable sensations, while ignoring the wretchedness beyond their boundary wall, would break up the moment they saw clearly into those other interiors. The world's habitation of cruelty will be dealt with in drastic fashion when the civilized peoples have had their vision."

V

The religious life is not one of mystic meditation. It is not absorption in dreams and visions. It is not the old ascetic idea of separation from the world, but it is knowing how to mix up in the world.

If we are religious at all, we are religious in the relationships of life. The Golden Rule is not a nice piece of sentiment for boys to learn in

Sunday school and then forget when they become business men. It is not a bit of impracticable idealism which men are to ignore in the fret and friction of every-day life.

It is the only rule that is practicable. It is the only rule that will work. We have tried the rule of gold, the rule of selfishness, we have tried culture and science and diplomacy, and according to a common verdict, "The future of our civilization looks black." We have tried everything else, and they only bring us to a blind alley. It is high time to give the Golden Rule a chance among men and to walk in the light of that "Light which lighteth every man coming into the world."

The multiplied relationships of to-day intensify the necessity of the Golden Rule. In other ages of the world, when nations dwelt apart in comparative independence of each other and the individual lived in isolation as a jack-of-all trades, there was not the same temptation to a violation of the spirit of justice, and there was not the same friction that followed this violation.

But to-day, in the complexity of modern life, our various relationships and points of contact have been so multiplied that we cannot go much farther unless the activities of our interrelated lives are harmonized by the principle of unselfishness.

VI

It is only the practice of the Golden Rule that will bring harmony to labor and capital.

A prominent political leader recently said, "A great deal of strife can be avoided if capitalists will take a human interest in their employees. It seems to us it would be wise for them to take as much interest in their workers as they do in their customers. If they applied the Golden Rule, I am sure there would be very few strikes."

On the other hand, if the employee applied the Golden Rule, he would do honest work and would avoid making unreasonable demands.

Politicians and hard-headed business men are at last coming into the conviction that the only way to industrial peace is the religious way.

In the business conducted by Mr. Arthur Nash the profits are shared with the workmen, the workers own one-third of the stock, and corporation has been changed to coöperation. When asked what he thought of it, a gentleman of distinctive Jewish accent replied: "Vot I tink of it, vot I tink of it? I am only sorry I did not tink of it first." Mr. Nash says: "I have come to the conclusion that all our economic troubles are due to a non-application of the Golden Rule, which is the only infallible, workable, industrial law in the universe."

There are some general principles having to

do with the application of the Golden Rule to industry, which by now should be generally accepted. I am not affirming that the business of Mr. Nash is in entire accord with the Golden Rule, but I think we must give him credit for making a sincere effort in that direction.

1. *There should be conceded the right of labor in collective bargaining.*

A well-known teacher of sociology in one of our universities makes a criticism of this demand of labor. "It denies to the employer the inalienable right to buy his labor in an open market."

A few years ago this professor was on the side of the great prophets: then gradually a metallic note crept into his voice and he is now on the side of large profits.

A discriminating judge has said: "There can be no freedom of contract where there is not equality of opportunity on both sides."

What ghost of a show has the isolated individual laborer against a close compact organization of capital?

I do not speak as a partisan of capital or labor; I am no expert on matters of technique in industrial management; but unless there is fair play in these chaotic days, we will "sow the wind and reap the whirlwind."

The corporations are entitled to honest work. The laborers are entitled to fair wages.

2. *There should be given to labor some part in the management of the enterprise.*

The laborers whose life and welfare are at stake should have some share in the control of organized industries. They are very vitally affected by the length of the working day and the sanitary conditions under which they work.

There must necessarily be a gradual change from the autocracy of the past to the coming democracy.

An English economist insists that without industrial democracy the forms of political democracy have availed but little and never will, since the beneficiaries of industrial privilege virtually own and actually control the State.

Despite the wild radicalism of much of the French Encyclopedia, we can hardly take issue with this statement: "A man's most sacred property is his labor. It is anterior even to the right of property, for it is the possession of those who own nothing else, so he must be sure to make the best of it he can."

President Wilson, in speaking before the American Federation of Labor, said: "I am speaking of my own experience when I say that the laborers are more reasonable in a larger number of cases than the capitalists."

Mr. John D. Rockefeller, Jr., has put the matter well: "Surely it is not consistent for us

Americans to demand democracy in government and practice autocracy in industry."

3. *The workmen should share in the profits.* This will tend to the distribution of wealth and the prevention of dangerous extremes in society.

The Federal Commission on Industrial Relations divides the population into three sections:

First, the rich, with two per cent of the population, own sixty per cent of the wealth.

Second, the middle class, with thirty-three per cent of the population, own thirty-five per cent of the wealth.

Third, the poor constitute sixty-five per cent of the population, with five per cent of the wealth.

At the top of the social scale luxury produces the same waste as poverty does at the bottom; disease, degeneracy, and false standard of living.

It is a case in which extremes meet in similar forms of viciousness and depravity.

A society which produces these extremes cannot be said to rest on a just basis.

In all this there is no cheap appeal to class prejudice. There is always the rage of envy on the part of the down and outs. The man who makes his money honestly and spends it generously is worth more than all his envious detractors.

But the industrial autocrat produces the Bolshevist, the I. W. W., and the selfish profiteer.

Anything is better than the red flag, but the only way to avoid it is to place business on a just basis. Chaplain Tiplady makes the pertinent statement: "Bolshevism is rampant in the world to-day, and cannot be destroyed by repression. It must be stamped out by the application of Christianity to business and industry. The Church must decide whether the social wrongs of the present age are to be dealt with by religion or revolution."

4. *There should be a reasonable limitation of working hours.* Every activity of body or mind uses up some physical tissues, which must be removed from the body and replaced by new tissues. In employments where the labor is monotonous and strenuous, the hours of labor should be fewer than in the more pleasant occupations.

Investigations have shown that some steel workers have worked twelve hours a day and for seven days in a week. In some instances there were twenty-four hours of continuous service when the change from day to night work took place.

Excessive toil results in fatigue and the perils that accompany fatigue. It has been abundantly demonstrated that fatigue weakens both physical resistance against disease and moral resistance against vice.

It has been proved by actual experiment that men have produced more products and better products in fewer hours. There is likewise the tendency at least to produce better men.

The committee of churchmen, under the leadership of Bishop F. J. McConnell, who were instrumental in reducing the excessive hours of labor were condemned even by other churchmen as meddlers.

5. *There should be the protection of childhood from industrial oppression and cruelty.* It appears that such a humane and Christian principle would be readily accepted by all, but we must reckon with the statement of Macaulay that the doctrine of gravitation would not yet be accepted if it had interfered with vested interests.

There are now nine States in our Union which have no laws prohibiting all children under fourteen from working in both factories and stores. Over one million children from ten to sixteen years are working in the United States in factories, mills, mines, canneries, agriculture, and other occupations. Nearly four hundred thousand of them are less than fourteen years of age. More than four hundred thousand of the million children at work between the ages of ten and fifteen years are employed in non-agricultural occupations.

We are not to worship the doctrine of States' rights as a political fetish, for we have no right to cling stubbornly to States' rights unless the States are willing to do right.

We cannot begin to reconcile the present condition of child labor in the United States with the Golden Rule of Christ.

Are we to continue to allow the promise and possibility of childhood, the seed corn of the nation, to be sacrificed for gain?

> "They look up with their pale and sunken faces,
> And their look is dread to see,
> For they mind you of their angels in high places,
> With eyes turned on Deity.
> How long, they say, how long, O cruel nation,
> Will you stand to move the world on a child's heart,
> Stifle down with a mailed heel its palpitation,
> And tread onward to your throne amid the mart?
> Our blood splashes upward, O gold-heaper,
> And your purple shows your path,
> But the child's sob in the silence curses deeper
> Than the strong man in his wrath."

How long shall the slaughter of the innocents continue? Shall we remain content with this sacrifice?

Artemus Ward declared the Civil War must continue; and as an expression of his devotion to the cause, he was willing to sacrifice all of his wife's relatives.

Do our industrial leaders propose to carry on their business by the proxy sacrifice of children?

We are prepared to believe that Bishop C. D. Williams was speaking with soberness when he said: "There is enough social dynamite in the utterances of Jesus to blow to bits every tyranny and oppression, every wrong and injustice, however hoary with age and buttressed with custom and ancient privilege, under which humanity groans. Only the gospel of the kingdom normally works like leaven rather than like dynamite. It generally changes society by evolution rather than by revolution. It is constructive rather than destructive.''

The Church is not authorized to pass on certain technical matters in the management of industry. Preachers are not competent to decide in an offhand way the justice or injustice of the wages of employees. But there are certain definite Christian principles in the relationships of industry that the Church and ministry are under obligation to champion.

The representation is made that Jesus directed himself solely to the individual, whereas the antagonism that resulted in his death was provoked by his attack on corporate and vested interests. "You have made my Father's house a den of thieves."

There is a certain type of corporation manager who is very zealous for the simple gospel.

The preacher is to keep his eye on heaven, while the corporation is to keep its eye on the main chance in this mundane sphere. There are corporations that would stifle the conscience of the preacher by saying to him, "You leave the mooted industrial question to us, and we will see to it that you receive an earthly reward in addition to your heavenly reward." One only has to know a little history to know what has happened with the policy of no interference and "hands off."

When Lord Shaftesbury introduced his legislation for regulating factories and mines with the purpose of preventing the exploitation of women and children, he met the most bitter antagonism, not only of the politicians, but of the Church and of nearly the whole bench of bishops in the House of Lords.

All legislation for industrial reform, including safety devices and enactments for social and industrial justice, has generally met the determined opposition of corporations.

There are Churchmen who profess to dwell in a lofty spiritual atmosphere and who discard all problems of labor and capital. This was not the way of the old prophets. Their words fairly blaze with indignant protest:

"They built up Zion with blood."

"Let judgment roll down as waters, and righteousness as a mighty stream."

It was not the way of Jesus when he thundered against those "who devoured widows' houses." The cry for the simple gospel has been made identical with a thin and emasculated gospel.

A prominent Church leader said: "The

worker does not need more labor laws; he needs more of God." But what is the objection of having both more just and democratic laws and more of God?

It seems more probable that the workman laboring under just and humane conditions would receive God into his life, than would the laborer who nurses bitterness from a sense of injustice.

VII

There is the application of the Golden Rule to freedom of speech. That right has been accentuated by what is known as the spy system in certain large industries, and also by the controversies that have been carried on as regards certain political and religious questions.

1. Growing out of the hysteria of fear produced by the World War, some thirty-four States and territories passed "Anti-sedition" laws directed against certain economic and political beliefs. Almost everybody was seeing "red" and thinking "red."

As a part of the reactionary movement the fight against freedom of speech was waged against the teacher and the preacher. The desire to protect political and ecclesiastical orthodoxy went far beyond any desire to protect living men from wrong and injustice. The declaration in our Constitution has been ignored: "Congress shall make no law respecting an establishment of religion, or prohibiting the free exercise thereof, or abridging the freedom of speech, or of the press."

All class government is opposed to freedom of speech. Bolshevism is class government. Lenine, an arch-priest of this political heresy, said: "We are going to smite the journals with fines and shut them up, arrest the editors and hold them as hostages."

Autocracy is class government and has lengthened out its hideous existence by suppressing free speech.

Buckle, the English historian, says: "In the period from the sixth to the tenth century there were not in all Europe more than three or four men who dared to think for themselves, and even they were obliged to veil their meaning in obscure and mystical language. Under these circumstances the few who were able to read confined their studies to works which encouraged and strengthened their superstitions."

An essential element of democracy is the right of free speech.

2. It may not be possible to draw a distinct line between liberty and license as regards speech.

There is the law against libel which is followed by penalty. No man can reasonably appeal to the principle of freedom to justify profane or obscene language. Freedom of speech does not include the right to incite to disobedience of law. There are the modifying terms in the Constitution, "peaceably" and to "petition the government."

There are certain limitations recognized by reason and common-sense discrimination that apply to incendiary and treasonable utterances.

It is not permissible to incite to murder. In a democracy there are legal means for removing grievances, so that any inducement to violence is not permitted.

If a citizen assert his freedom in expressing treasonable utterances, the State has a right to say, "You are perfectly free to say what you please, but the State is perfectly free to see to it that you exercise this freedom somewhere outside the State."

If a preacher should assert his freedom in antagonizing fundamental doctrines of Christianity, the Church has a right to say, "You are perfectly free to say what you please, but the Church is perfectly free to see to it that you exercise this freedom somewhere outside the Church."

3. A reasonable reserve should be cultivated. No man should feel constrained to make a constant exposure of his mental insides. But barring an undue license of speech, there must be conceded the right of freedom. To suppress forcibly all erroneous utterances would be the

worst possible damage that could happen. The errors festering within are more dangerous both to the individual and society.

The friction of minds produces light. It is better to express opinions that are false, that they may be rectified in the rough and tumble of discussion, than to suppress opinions that are true through considerations of cowardly prudence. The man who is mistaken, but who is true to the truth as he sees it, will come into possession of the living truth. The man who is in possession of the truth but represses it, will have at last only the dry bones of truth stripped of flesh and blood. Freedom of discussion is based not on the supposition that everybody is right, but on the fact that everybody is wrong in some particular ideas, with the possibility of these errors being corrected.

4. Our safety and progress are involved in this principle of freedom.

Dr. Hugh Black says, as regards the Church: "The Church, in seeking to satisfy the intellect, should not be afraid of controversy. Indeed we should welcome it. There is a false peace in intellectual life as elsewhere which consists in creating a desert and calling it peace. In every other sphere of knowledge, progress comes by criticism, by fearless disputes. Untrammeled discussion is the only safeguard of truth. When we recognize that truth is an ideal which we can only hope to approximate, we are not distressed by comparative failure. The early Church acquired its theology by free discussion. We must seek to shape our system of thought by translating into modern language and modern thought the doctrines of faith. To do this we should grant willingly and gladly freedom to investigate and to think. We who believe in the triumph of truth may well believe in such freedom."

Furthermore, failure always follows the fallacy of physical force. The most dangerous idea is the one that is suppressed. It has all the explosive qualities of dynamite. Make a martyr of the false or foolish agitator and forthwith a number of people will steadfastly believe that he is the paragon of wisdom and truth. Let him talk until his tongue lolls out and his utterances begin to sound like the ravings of lunacy.

Judge Oliver Wendell Holmes, of the U. S. Supreme Court, said: "It is with effervescing opinions as with the not yet forgotten champagnes, the quickest way to let them get flat is to let them get exposed to the air."

Mr. Jefferson expressed his faith in the inherent strength of free government in the following words: "If there be any among us who wish to dissolve the union, or to change its republican form, let them stand undisturbed as monuments of the safety with which error of opinion may be tolerated, where reason is left free to combat it."

5. The only way to fight error is with truth. The only way to overcome darkness is with light.

The classic statements on freedom of speech are made by Milton and Mill.

Milton in his "Areopagitica" writes: "We cannot call the forceful suppression of error wisdom, since the corruptions which it seeks to prevent break in faster at other doors which cannot be shut. Though all the winds of doctrine were let loose to play upon the earth, so truth be in the field, we do injuriously by licensing and prohibiting to misdoubt her strength. Let her and falsehood grapple; who ever knew truth put to the worse in a free and open encounter?"

There are three propositions given by Mill that are stated in substance which express the advantages of freedom of thought and speech.

First, the received opinion may be false, and some other opinion consequently true. In this instance the suppression of liberty of discussion deprives people of the opportunity of exchanging error for truth.

Second, the received opinion may be true and the opposing opinion false. In this case, the prohibition of free speech to the opposition deprives people of that clearness in the apprehension of truth which comes from conflict with error. Unless the received opinion, even though true, is suffered to be vigorously contested, it will for the most part be held in the manner of a prejudice with little feeling of its rational ground. It is in danger of becoming a mere dogma without any real and heartfelt conviction.

Third, the conflicting doctrines may share the truth between them. Neither opinion is wholly true or wholly false. The nonconforming opinion is needed to supply the remainder of the truth, of which the received doctrine embodies only a part. Since the prevailing opinion is rarely the whole truth, it is only by the collision of adverse opinions that the remainder of the truth has any chance of being supplied. So in this instance to suppress the nonconforming opinion is to deprive people of the whole truth.

Viscount Bryce, in his epoch-marking work, "Modern Democracies," says: "Free discussion will sift all statements. All arguments will be heard and canvassed. The people will know how to choose the sound and reject the unsound. They may be for a time misled, but general freedom will work out better than any kind of restraint. In free countries no one now impeaches the principle, whether or not he expects from it all it seems to promise. The liberty of the press remains an Ark of the Covenant in every democracy."

In many of our great dailies the proprietors

keep an ear to the ground and speak softly but firmly into the ears of editors.

A great daily must have abundant advertisements. To secure the advertisements and make them remunerative there must be a large subscription list. The proprietor must feel the pulse beat of advertisers and subscribers, and the editor must feel the purse beat of the proprietor. "When the opinions of a journal begin to count, it ceases to have opinions."

It is equally true that when the opinions of some politicians and preachers begin to count they cease to have opinions and merely repeat the shibboleths of the established order that they may have a safer tenure in their established position.

The progress of society, the State, and the Church has always been conditioned on the pioneers who blazed the pathway which must be walked in because they were willing to think differently.

VIII

There is to be the application of the Golden Rule in social service. There is the call not only for justice, but for mercy.

If from the time your eyes first opened on the light you were doomed to abject poverty, in an atmosphere of crime and immorality, with the handicaps of ignorance and disease, with scarcely a fighting chance in life, with the heavy weights both of evil heredity and evil environment, do you not think from your present viewpoint that you would want some strong and sympathetic persons to bring you help in your hopeless struggle? Then it is for you to carry help and hope to such a life.

This divine principle is well expressed by a recent writer: "I believe that babies everywhere should be as well-born and kindly tended as I would have my own; that motherhood should be protected as I would have the mother that is dearest to me; that childhood should be as joyous and youth as free to come to its own as mine should be if I could have my wish; that womanhood should be guarded everywhere with the chivalry that I would give my best; that every man's labor should be as honored and as fairly estimated as I want mine to be; that all lives should be lightened and blessed with the leisure that I enjoy for myself; that the higher human values for which I crave should be available for all mankind; that every man's future should be cared for as I would have my own; and that everyone everywhere should have the love and kindly esteem and generous appreciation that I desire so keenly for myself."

A selfish individualism has no slightest support in the teaching of Jesus. He held that wealth only fulfilled its purpose in the welfare of humanity. He held that the true gold of earth was humanity and that according to the divine estimate "one of these little ones" was of inestimable value. That man, however technically honest and outwardly respectable and upright, who ignores his debt to the unprivileged has not lived according to the principles of Jesus.

A man of large wealth died some years ago, leaving no legacy to any worthy enterprise. His name is a very familiar one, and many of our readers doubtless know the nameless person to whom reference is made. His poor defense for his selfishness is to the effect that he refused to do any generous thing lest he might be thought vain. He preferred to gorge his three heirs with wealth rather than minister in any way to his people who had made his fortune possible.

If all men of wealth were like this man, the United States would be red in a decade. He was not only false to the spirit of all the teaching of Jesus on stewardship, but he set an example of selfishness which, if generally followed to-day, would inevitably result in red-handed revolution. Men in general, irrespective of religion, believe that the possessors of wealth owe a debt to society, and wealth has permanent security only as it pays the debt. Those of smaller possessions owe this debt, and it is a fearful failure to appear before the bar of divine justice without having paid it.

It is refreshing to turn to a contrast. Leland Stanford lost his only child, and while he was one of the United States Senators from California he was once saying to himself, "I have nothing to live for. I have no children." He put a million dollars into a private home, but it was not a home to him. One night in a dream his son appeared to him and said: "Father, never say again you have nothing to live for—live for humanity, live for other peoples' children." There soon arose at Palo Alto the Leland Stanford Junior University at a cost of $20,000,000. He and Mrs. Stanford became the devoted Christian servants of the poor, the orphan, and the suffering and left all their property to go on doing good to the rising generations.

We can well afford to pray that many other men might dream dreams like this and practice their dreams as did Leland Stanford.

The only sin we find in Dives, who lifted up his eyes in hell, is that he was a selfish individualist.

James Russell Lowell put this sin in memorable verse in his "Parable." He tells how our Lord determined to come back to earth to see "how the men my brethren believe in me." Great preparations were made to receive him.

The scribes and Pharisees and rulers of the day did everything that they could think of to do him royal honor. Costly carpets were spread for his feet. Great organs poured forth their noble music. He was shown the magnificent churches and cathedrals and the images of himself that they had reared. But the Saviour walked with downcast eyes and sorrowful countenance. He could hear the groans of the forgotten, the oppressed. At last He spoke:

> "Have ye founded your thrones and altars, then,
>   On the bodies and souls of living men?
>   And think ye that building shall endure
>   Which shelters the noble and crushes the poor?
>
> With gates of silver and bars of gold
>   Ye have fenced my sheep from their Father's fold;
>   I have heard the dropping of their tears
>   In heaven these eighteen hundred years."
>
> Then Christ sought out an artisan,
>   A low-browed, stunted, haggard man,
>   And a motherless girl, whose fingers thin
>   Pushed from her faintly want and sin.
>
> These set He in the midst of them,
>   And as they drew back their garment-hem
>   For fear of defilement, "Lo, here," said he,
> "The images ye have made of me."

CHAPTER V

THE GOLDEN RULE (Concluded)

There has been stressed the fact of our social obligation in relieving the physical wretchedness of people. All schemes of material improvement are good as far as they go, but they do not go far enough.

You may have your regulations for pure food and sanitary milk for the children, and reasonable hours and fair wages for the laborer. All of these should be done. And yet you have not solved the economic problem, for we have no guarantee that men will provide for their families, and that poverty and wretchedness will be removed. What security have we against the expenditure of money in sin, debauchery, licentiousness, and gambling, except a change of purpose, a renewed will, a transformation of the inner spirit? Our self-mastery is through our Master, even Christ.

There is no possibility of advancing the interests of labor without reckoning with the moral issues involved. We will not attempt to make any discriminating estimate of the two counter statements: "Poverty produces drunkenness, and drunkenness produces poverty." What we are now contending for is the self-evident proposition that drunkenness produces much poverty. We are gratified to know that this is being recognized by labor. Forty-five per cent of the labor leaders in England are strictly temperate. John Burns, a leading labor leader of England, says: "One-half of the problem of the unemployed in England is caused by intemperance."

This leads us to the next proposition.

I

The Golden Rule will lead you to a spiritual ministry.

If you are conscious that you have a possession in Jesus Christ that is the supreme need of every man who is without it, then you are under obligation to share the high spiritual value with such a life.

It is here that we are to find our strong motive in our whole missionary endeavor.

If you were in total spiritual darkness, without the light of Jesus Christ, without God and without hope in the world, looking at the question from your viewpoint of advantage, would you not want some Christlike spirit to bring you the gospel message with its wealth of comfort and inspiration?

THE GOLDEN RULE

When we experience the riches of Christ in our lives, we can say without any sort of cant that, compared with him, the wealth of the world is but gaudy tinsel. Then we know that what Jesus Christ is to our own spirits, he can be to every one who believes in him.

> "O what delights can equal those
> That stir the spirit's inner deeps,
> When one who loves and knows not reaps
> A truth from one who loves and knows?"

II

The Golden Rule must be conscientiously applied to the interracial relationship of life. The divine principle involves the payment of the debt that strength owes to weakness. It frees the privileged life from cruelty and contempt. If I were a foreigner, I am sure I would prefer being called an Italian or a Chinaman rather than a "Dago" or a "Chink."

If I were a negro, I think I would recognize and adapt myself to my social position; but I am sure I would not want my inferiority thrust at me like an open knife. I am sure I would not want "nigger," with a tone of reflection that comes from a peculiar inflection, constantly rubbed in on my sensibilities. I would want to be treated with fairness and justice. What

I would not want done to me, I must not do to others.

There has been the disposition on the part of many white people to fall into such a fear over the bugaboo of social equality that they fail to exercise toward the negro common justice.

Sam was asked to go on an errand that carried him by the graveyard and he said: "No suh, boss, I ain't gwine by dar; I'se skeerd of dem ghosts." "O, Sam, don't you know ghosts can't hurt you?" "Yes, suh, I knows ghosts can't hurt you, but dey sho kin make you hurt yo'self."

The ghost of social equality results in some people hurting themselves.

The leading representatives, with the large majority of each race, fully agree on these two considerations; there should be no social equality and there should be racial integrity. One has to practice only ordinary observation to see that our peril is not social equality among the higher elements of the races, but sexual equality among the lower elements of the races. As a race develops, there is a growth of racial consciousness and of the ideal of racial integrity. Each race has its peculiar contribution to make to the common treasure of humanity, and this contribution can only be made by maintaining racial integrity. What the far future may hold—that is too remote for specu-

THE GOLDEN RULE

lation—we cannot say, but the pathway of our present program for the good of all races is clearly evident.

The mixture of the races either by mixed marriage or illicit relationship must be stoutly opposed. The tragedy of this intermingling is for the negro the most pitiable one in human history.

The fear of social equality on the part of the white race has resulted in a failure very many times to do the negro justice as a human being and an American citizen.

The unreasonable and nervous anxiety as regards negro domination magnifies unduly the strength of the negro race.

Booker Washington facetiously remarked: "The negro race is stronger than the white race, since it takes one hundred per cent of white blood to make a white man, while one per cent of negro blood makes a negro."

We are under every obligation of honor to treat the negro fairly, since our own forefathers invited the negro to come and live with us, and the invitation was given in such an urgent and even coercive way that it was not possible for the negro to refuse the invitation. Under these circumstances it is mean and contemptible to withhold from the negro the largest possibility for his own racial progress. The people who pride themselves on one hundred per cent Americanism are certainly much less than one hundred per cent American, unless they are willing that every black child should have the opportunity of an education and a fair chance in the world.

When Simon Peter hesitated in answering a call to minister to a man of another race, he was led by the Spirit of God into his great declaration, "Of a truth I perceive that God is no respecter of persons."

The ideal of racial integrity is normal and justifiable, but racial prejudice and enmity are abnormal and un-Christian.

Racial prejudice and enmity, instead of being in reality instinctive, appear to be transmitted by social heredity and as a matter of cultivation, as is illustrated in the attitude of small children.

A Southern white man is quoted as having said: "I ain't got nothing agin' the nigger. I was fourteen years old before I knew I was better than a nigger."

As difficult as the task is, we must strive as earnestly against race prejudice as we strive to maintain racial integrity. Bishop A. G. Haygood was speaking out of his own experience when he said: "Race prejudice—it is harder than quartz; who can break it? It is colder than the icebergs of the Arctics; who can melt it?"

No man of a stronger race can deliberately inflict an injury on a member of a weaker race without inflicting a double injury upon his own life.

The frail fingers of the weakest child of God whom you wrong can bar forever against you the gates of gold, even though those frail fingers are black.

III

The Golden Rule is the only workable rule in our international relations. The solidarity of our modern world with its interrelationship and interdependence makes the application of the Golden Rule imperative. The whole world is so tied together that it is not so much one neighborhood as a vast apartment house, where a destructive fire in one room is of much concern to all the occupants. Even the cry of an infant in one room may be of such interest as to drive slumber away from a disinterested party in another room.

Some sort of international agreement, some form of a league of nations is a vital necessity. Our only hope in a league of nations is not through confidence in the mere power of organization, but in making possible the application of the Golden Rule to strong and weak nations alike. Some people prate about a league of nations as if its purpose were to force their sons to fight across the seas. But when there was no league of nations our boys were forced across the seas to engage in a fight which is said to have had its origin in a disagreement about pigs. Servia became enraged because Austria discriminated against her in favor of Hungary in the shipment of pigs. Whether this is accurate or not, we know that the immediate occasion of the war was about a little piece of pig-headed royalty. In more than 3,000 years of recorded history all were years of war except 237 years. This happened without a league of nations. No, the sole purpose and that which will be the result of a just league of nations is to prevent war. It is your Triple Ententes and Triple Alliances and secret diplomacy which constitute the hotbed in which the war spirit thrives. These are the entangling alliances which Washington was able to foresee. To make a misapplication of "entangling alliances" marks a man not only as a standpatter but as a hopeless reactionary who uses the past not for a guidepost but for a hitching post. Practically every argument used against the Constitution and federation of the States has been repeated against any form of a league of nations.

We are confronted by a dangerous reaction in the realm of the spirit, in the realm of an unselfish idealism. Human nature is so weak that,

THE GOLDEN RULE

when it reaches a high level, we begin to look for a moral slump. It is a long descent from the heroic spirit of our soldiers who went forth with the watchword, "America for the world," to the motto of some politicians of to-day, "America for herself first, and last, and all the time."

We can but hope that a large number of our people, very good people, are passing through only a transient mood of selfishness.

We must share our wealth with other nations. We must share our knowledge with other nations. Mexico needs missionaries and schoolteachers far more than our jingoism and guns.

We must share our power with other nations. We must make it impossible for one nation to pounce upon another without incurring the opposition of the rest of the world. Since the rest of the world would have to share the injurious effects of a war between even two nations, the rest of the world ought to be able to say whether it is going to happen or not.

The United States is under obligation to the extent of her power to see to it that another war shall not happen. It is not worth while to indulge in the unprofitable speculation of whether another war could be justified, but we are to set ourselves steadfastly against the further recurrence of the military mania.

We must loathe war and hate war, and strip

it of all its falseness and glamour and let it stand forth in its unveiled hideousness.

> "War
> I abhor,
> And yet how sweet
> The sound along the marching street
> Of drum and fife, and I forget
> Wet eyes of widows and forget
> Broken old mothers and the whole
> Dark butchery without a soul."

War is not the gay color, the rhythmic movement, the thrilling sensation of the military parade. War is murder, blood, agony, death and hell. War is murder of innocent women and children. War means physical mutilation and indescribable pain and death. "Its heroisms are but the glancing sunlight on a sea of blood."

War robs the future. The financial cost of the war was $337,000,000,000. This is enough money to have built a schoolhouse and a church within reach of every human being in the world, with a large surplus left for various benevolences. About 14,000,000 soldiers were killed. No one can estimate what this means, in the destruction of genius, art, literature, statesmanship, and religious leadership. All the years of all ages of human history have had to do with the making of every man. The loss is great and irreparable. He who kills a nightingale not only kills a nightingale, but all the nightingales that would have descended from this nightingale, and

THE GOLDEN RULE

which would have made melody through the years. That which kills a man not only kills a man, but all future descendants who would have added their wealth to the world. War kills the best, the strongest, and the most heroic. Millions of children living have been cheated out of a father's care and a child's chance in the world.

Dr. S. Parkes Cadman arraigns the false glorification of war. "The drill sergeant outdid the scholar and the cleric. The coarse, second-rate sentiments of junkers, bureaucrats, chauvinistic officials and journalists menaced the good will of nations. Few great thinkers or prophets received a thousandth part of the attention given to the ravings of militarism. Invocation to battle, and the triumph of the sword as the passport to all that honorably befits nations, were the stock tenets of nationalistic barbarism. Even the poetry and the drama of our yesterdays are full of hacking and hewing; of gold-braided uniforms, blood, and gunpowder. They are grossly brutal, painfully monotonous, without a ray of human interest or sympathy to lighten the black shadows of their adoration of physical force. To butcher the foe is a heavenly enterprise, sanctioned by Churchmen who repealed the Sermon on the Mount for the sake of State Conquest and State Worship. These travesties upon Christianity registered the actual situation in Europe.

Her fate and that of half the world besides lay in the hands of a dozen men more suited to the tastes of Tamerlane than to civilized rulers. They had their day; then the seething volcano exploded, and now they have their night, which should be a long one. For us the weightiest conclusions are: first, that an international condition which could permit so stupendous a crime against the race was a negation of God; and second, that it is the inescapable obligation of Christians, and of all sane and moralized people, to prevent a repetition of the crime."

The Churches should speak out in the name of the Prince of Peace. General Bliss has said: "If another war like the last one should come, the professing Christians of the United States will be responsible for every drop of blood that will be shed and for every dollar wastefully expended."

1. There is the practical defense of war from the standpoint of profits. If our nation should stupidly stumble into another war, I want the first gas attack to be turned on the munition makers, bloated profiteers, jingo politicians, and commercial exploiters who hitherto have kept their full paunches out of the danger zone and made their purses full. I do not want anybody killed, but we would be prepared to part from these men with fewer regrets than any other class of citizens.

2. There is the theoretic defense of war on the part of certain theologians.

There is the theory of a crude Adventism which glorifies war as fulfilling prophecy and as being a herald of the approaching end of the world. They readily resign themselves to any amount of bloodshed, if they are allowed to interpret it as the fulfillment of some obscure prophecy. They have no hope for the world except in a kind of celestial militarism in which Jesus will be a Super-Kaiser.

There is again the preacher of the extreme individualistic type who holds to the inevitability of war until everybody is regenerated. This is a consummation devoutly to be wished, but the application is absurd.

They have in reality no hope for the cessation of war. It is the blackest pessimism to hold that war is a permanent institution. The ecclesiastical Bourbon, like the poor, is always with us. The Bourbon or junker type of mind never forgets anything that is old, nor learns anything new. Yes, they do forget some things, for duelling, slavery, and polygamy were once declared permanent institutions.

The ecclesiastical Bourbon only thinks that he thinks, and when he thinks that he is thinking, he is only making a rearrangement of his prejudices. He is in a worse situation than Rip Van Winkle, for Rip did wake up.

We are to war against war, not with the nerveless Hamlet, who said,

> "The time is out of joint, O, cursed spite,
> That ever I was born to set it right,"

but rather in the spirit of the militant soul of Rupert Brook as he sailed for Gallipoli: "Now, God be thanked who has matched us with this hour."

In the fine sentence of James, "We are to find the moral equivalent of war."

William James in his essay on "The Moral Equivalent of War" says: "War represents the strong life. Militarism is the great preserver of our ideals of hardihood. The warlike spirit has been bred in the bone. Man is a fighting animal. The military feelings are too deeply grounded to abdicate their place until better substitutes are offered." James proposes as a substitute social service. Dr. Samuel McCrea Cavert claims that a world missionary enterprise is the only task big enough and universal enough in its appeal to take the place of war. There is a uniqueness in the expression of Mr. James, but the idea itself is in a very old Book, where we are exhorted "to war a good warfare" and "to fight the good fight of faith." Milton says to Cromwell: "Much remains to conquer still. Peace hath her victories no less renowned than war."

THE GOLDEN RULE

Prof. Francis G. Peabody gives these strong words: "It is a brave thing to be a soldier; but may it not be a still braver thing to be a Saviour? It needs a still greater courage to take the sword of the Spirit. Ought not the time then soon come when the application of the fighting instinct to the brutalities of bloodshed will be recognized as a base prostitution of one of the noblest traits of human nature, from which real men will turn with disgust to the real wars of creative tasks; and when the famous names of warfare will be not those of great generals who have depopulated hostile lands, but of the greater generals who have directed the armies of science and healing, of public service and the amelioration of life, to beneficent and coöperative ends? The instincts of militarism cannot be destroyed, but they can be fulfilled, and the victories of the battlefield may be supplanted by that self-effacing and creative heroism which shall have the right to sing the hymn of triumph, 'Thanks be to God, who giveth us the victory through our Lord Jesus Christ.' The spirit of militarism must be converted to the spirit of service and the battles of the future won by the sword of the Spirit."

The moral equivalent of war is to be found in both a world-wide missionary enterprise and also the multiplied forms of service for humanity. There must be the evangelization of those who are without the gospel and the Christianizing of human relationships.

We are to disregard the cheap sneer of extreme individualism at Christianizing relationships. Philemon, the master, and Onesimus, the slave, both became Christians. But the relationship between master and slave was never Christianized until the slave became free.

IV

This leads me in the last place to state something of what I conceive to be the true idea of Christian perfection, that perfection which puts into practice the Golden Rule and carries out the duties and obligations of personal relationships. There are men of saintly lives, the latchet of whose shoes I am not worthy to unloose, who hold what appears to me to be very imperfect ideas of perfection.

No subject has been discussed with such imperfection of method and spirit as Christian Perfection. Men have fussed about it and quarreled over theories and displayed a very imperfect temper. Men have come to hate each other over a difference of opinion concerning perfect love.

There has been the failure to recognize the difference in religious temperament. There has been the effort to cast various temperaments into the same mold.

There has been the mistake of seeking support for a theory in the theology of some of the fathers, rather than in the Scriptures and in the teaching of Jesus.

Controversialists have quoted the Methodist fathers differently according to their own bias instead of appealing to the Word of authority.

There has been the mistake of dealing in the abstract rather than in the concrete, in introspection rather than personal interrelationship. There results a morbidness and an ingrowing conscience. Men have theorized about the first blessing, the second blessing, the third blessing, the inbred sin, the Adamic taint, the remnants of the old man, and have indulged in an introspective analysis.

We are on the right road to perfection, when we get out into the free open air of personal relationship and rightly relate ourselves to God and to our fellow men.

Christian progress comes through bringing more and more of our acts under the sway of the Christian spirit and more and more persons under the influence of our expression of that spirit.

Bishop F. J. McConnell writes: "The New Testament teaches an ideal of perfect life like that of God himself. And the struggle for the ideal is to find itself not only in inner sanctification but in outer goodness of conduct. God sends rain and sunshine upon the evil and the good. Even-handed impartiality is one of the works of the perfection of God; and the implication of the New Testament teaching is that it is characteristic of the goodness of God that he recognizes and acts upon obligations to all men, good and bad. If we can imagine a sphere of relations to men which would be indifferent to God, we might have valid excuse for stopping outside of some circles of human contact, as if these were religiously indifferent to us. The New Testament doctrine of entire sanctification is that we are to carry the sanctifying spirit into all departments of life. If we draw lines beyond which we will not go, we must recognize that we are Christians only up to those boundary lines."

In the connection in which Jesus enjoins perfection, he is speaking of perfection in love and is laying stress upon the personal relationships of life.

There must be an extending sway of the spirit over widening and deepening relationships. There must be a growing love for God. There must be a growing love for people and a growing love for more people. In the circle of human relationships, love must be deepened and widened.

THE GOLDEN RULE

As to the matter of a profession of perfect love it will relieve you of presumption to leave the question of that attainment to a more impartial judge. A brother was making extravagant claims in an experience meeting. A brother in the audience said to one by his side: "Well, I can't say that." The reply was: "Oh, go on and say it; that is all he did."

When Jesus says, "Be ye perfect, even as your Father which is in heaven is perfect," he is speaking of perfection in love and is laying stress on the personal relationships of life.

Life's highest reach is in the realm of personal relationships. Life's highest power is exercised in the realm of personal relationships. We have felt the strengthening and sanctifying influence of a stalwart human character, and this transforming power reaches its consummation on our personal relationship to Jesus Christ. It is for persons, not for abstract ideas, that the heart hungers. The incident is given of a little girl who was left in her bed upstairs, as her mother kissed her good night and went down for the evening. To the child, afraid to be left alone, the mother said: "But, dearest, you are not alone. Your doll is here, and then you know that God is always with you." The child answered: "Yes, but even if I have my doll, and even if God is here, I want somebody with a skin face."

Browning puts in David's song to Saul the same wistful longing:

> "'Tis the weakness in strength, that I cry for! my flesh, that I seek
> In the Godhead! I seek and I find it. O Saul, it shall be
> A Face like my face that receives thee; a Man like to me,
> Thou shalt love and be loved by, forever: a Hand like this hand
> Shall throw open the gates of new life to thee! See the Christ stand!"

Life can only be perfected by carrying the Christly spirit into human relationships, in the family, in the Church, in the State, in social life, and among members of other races and other nations. All of these multiplied relationships are God's wondrous mill for turning out the finished product.

They constitute his gymnasium for the building up of character. There is the mistaken notion of a good life apart from these relationships. But the hermit who has tried to work out his salvation in loneliness of life has found more delusions and devils besieging his mind than all the human beings put together.

Men are prone to make the complaint that if it were not for some human beings they could get along first rate.

As well might the fish complain that it could swim if it were not for the water. As well might the bird complain that it could fly if it

THE GOLDEN RULE

were not for the air. These human relationships with the spirit that does the Christly thing are absolutely necessary for completing human life.

It is only with other human beings that we can practice the Golden Rule.

"It is the Golden Rule of Christ that will bring in the golden age of man."

CHAPTER VI

ORTHODOXY AND OBEDIENCE

I

A PRACTICAL obedience to the principles of Jesus Christ is an expression and at the same time an evidence of a vital faith.

It makes no difference how orthodox you are if that is all. "The devils believe and tremble." You may believe that Jesus said "Love your enemies" and never practice it.

You may believe in the atonement of Jesus Christ and never suffer for one sinning soul. You may accept the incarnation and yet never incarnate a single distinctive principle in your own life. You may believe that God doeth all things well and yet do nothing well yourself. There are those who allow the worship of the Son of God to take the place of following the Son of God.

The controversy as to which is more important, doctrine or life, creed or conduct, has a similarity to the question as to which is more necessary, air or water. It may be said once for all that the man who underestimates the value of doctrine falls into the mistake of ignoring the vital relation between belief and conduct. Jesus, in picturing the final judgment scene in Matthew xxv., lays stress on practical service. However, those who won his approval evidently had faith in God and in their needy fellow men as children of God.

Doctrine is important, because it is important to believe the truth and because it was the mission of Jesus to bear witness to the truth.

The element of faith, however, does not involve perfection in the definitions and technicalities of a system of doctrine. It is doubtless true, as has been well said, that if all Christian men for the next twenty years would give up the attempt to explain Christ and devote their attention to following him, at the end of that time they would know more about the person of Christ than they had ever known before, and they would have put Christianity in a position to conquer the world.

The common attitude toward the Bible is too largely sentimental. There are plenty of people who are ready to heap upon the Bible empty compliments. They make their boast of the Bible and glory in the land of the open Bible, while their Bibles remain closed. They abuse the Roman Catholic Church for withholding the Bible from the people, while they own a Bible, but do not read it. People consider it an appropriate marriage gift, an excellent lesson book for children, a good book to read to the sick, a good book to preach from in the pulpit, and a beautiful ornament for the parlor. People are ready to defend the Bible, but in the rush of modern life they do not read it. Men call it God's book and divine, but they repeat but empty terms if they do not bring to bear upon it their powers of thought and study. The great message of God's revelation is crowded out with every other sort of literature. There are men who never touch a Bible except when they take an oath in a law court. There are women who never touch the Bible except when they dust it, or transfer it to another table or shelf.

The Bible does not need our defense, but we need the defense which it will give us amid life's perils. John Ruskin has said to his own English people: "You are all shrieking now with one voice because you hear of your Bible being attacked. If you choose to obey your Bible, you will never care who attacks it. It is just because you never fulfill a single downright precept of the Book that you are so careful for its credit; and it is because you don't care to obey the whole words that you are so particular about the letters. The Bible tells you to dress plainly, and you are mad for finery; the Bible tells you to have pity on the poor, and you crush them be-

ORTHODOXY AND OBEDIENCE 129

neath your chariot wheels; the Bible tells you to do judgment and justice, and you do not know nor care to know so much as what the Bible word justice means."

There is a mutilation of the Scriptures on the part of certain traditionalists that is as indefensible as the method of radical critics. A Church editor writes: "Each man's real Bible is the amount of the Bible that he is trying to live. What he knows, simply to dispute over with other folks who do not read the book exactly as he does, has no Bible value to him. What he sees to be livable and what he honestly wants to put into practice, that is surcharged for him with the veritable inspiration of God. And he can make a bigger Bible for himself with a surer inspiration if he will search the Scriptures for more and more that he can tie to and live by."

It is a fearful mutilation of the Bible when a man, whatever may be his theory, practically excludes the Golden Rule. The man who refuses to live according to the principles of the Sermon on the Mount has been guilty of a dangerous elimination. What shall be said of the man who mutilates the Scriptures by practically ignoring "Thou shalt love thy neighbor as thyself." There are rabid traditionalists who stickle for the letter and become violent in their language against all legitimate investigation and leave completely out the thirteenth chapter of Corinthians. Without any compunction they cut out the admonition concerning "Speaking the truth in love." They do not speak the truth and do not speak in love. The man who eliminates truth and love from the Divine Revelation is cutting the heart out and is guilty of a fatal mutilation of the Scriptures.

Beyond any question the Bible teaches us to love the truth and not to be afraid of it and to cultivate the spirit of love. If you are not going to hold to the heart of the Scripture and practice it, then you have no use for any of it. We may best understand the word by doing the word. There is wonderfully illuminating power in a good deed. We can really understand the high command, "Love your enemies," only as we practice it. We can never understand "It is more blessed to give than to receive" unless we practice it. We can find out the fullness of God's will only as we do his will up to our understanding. The good will is a wonderful interpreter of God's requirements, because it is willing to do them. The hearer of the word who is not a doer of the word is a forgetful hearer, and "forgets what manner of man he is." "He that willeth to do his will shall know the doctrine."

The use of the true method of interpretation which involves the intellect, the sensibility, and

ORTHODOXY AND OBEDIENCE

the will, results in a sane interpretation of the Holy Scriptures. Thus the true method of interpretation frees the Bible from hurtful misunderstandings and perversions, removes stumblingblocks out of the way of Christian faith, and gives more light to the sacred page, making it radiant with the Divine Presence.

Just before President Harding passed into the new life, in almost his last address to his fellow men, he uttered these memorable words: "I tell you, my countrymen, the world needs more of the Christ; the world needs the spirit of the Man of Nazareth. If we could bring into the relationships of humanity, among ourselves and among the nations of the earth, the brotherhood that was taught by the Christ, we would have a restored world; we would have a new hope for humanity throughout the globe." Would you have an infallible guide, one on whom you can always depend? Then accept Christ as the Way. Make his teachings, his life, and his abiding spirit your guide, and you will become living testimonies to the truth of his promise. "I am the light of the world; he that followeth me shall not walk in darkness, but shall have the light of life."

The real test of the Christian life does not consist in profession, or creed, or Church attendance, but in doing the will of God as revealed in Jesus Christ. One of my revered teachers when in London went to hear Spurgeon and was curious to know his method of dividing his topic into propositions.

After announcing his text Mr. Spurgeon said: "I wish to discuss three propositions from the text. First, before coming to church: 'Laying aside all wickedness and superfluity of naughtiness.' Second, while at church: 'Receive with meekness the engrafted word, which is able to save your souls.' Third, after leaving church: 'Be ye doers of the word, and not hearers only, deceiving your own selves.'"

It is easy to look pious and feel pious while at church. I have often wished for a picture of a congregation at church. They would look like a group of angels. But how about the following week when they mix up with the rough and tumble and pell-mell affairs of everyday life?

It is easier to die for the faith than to live for it. St. Paul tells us that a man will die for the faith without the high motive of love.

There is the meditative and mystic element in religion. The wealth of motive power springs out of faith in the Spiritual and Supernatural. There is the divine side of what God, through Jesus Christ and the Holy Spirit, can do for you. There is the contrasted conception of what you can do for God. It is only the practical Christianity that gives strength and sanity to reli-

ORTHODOXY AND OBEDIENCE

gious faith and prevents it from being or becoming an idle dreaminess and a vague mysticism.

The test of character is in what we do. In the "Merchant of Venice" Portia says: "If to do good were as easy as to know what were good to be done, chapels had been churches, and poor men's cottages princes' palaces. It is a good divine that follows his own instructions. I can easier teach twenty what were good to be done, than to be one of the twenty to follow mine own teaching. The brain may devise laws for the blood, but a hot temper leaps o'er a cold decree."

There is the story of a gentleman who was traveling in England, and who was sitting on the box with the driver of a coach. He observed that one of the horses seemed to be shirking his part of the work. He remarked to the driver: "That horse does not seem to draw much." The driver said: "Not an inch, sir." He replied: "Why then do you have him?" The answer was: "Well, you see, sir, this is a four-horse coach, and he counts for one of them." Some people are counted who do not contribute anything of real service to the Church.

In contrast with this, Mr. Beecher while riding with a friend observed that one of the horses was doing most of the work, showing much spirit and a dogged perseverance. He then remarked on this fact to the driver, who replied: "Yes, he is doing more than he should." Then Mr.

Beecher added: "Well, I wish that horse was a member of my Church."

There is no place in the Church for the shirker, hardly any for the jerker, but urgent call all the time for the sure and steady worker.

The final art in the cultivation of a Christian character is practice. That practice makes perfect is true in the religious realm. Theories alone can get us nowhere.

> We learn to walk by walking—
> We learn to swim by swimming—
> We learn to fly by flying—
> We learn to paint by painting—
> We learn to write by writing—
> We learn to sing by singing—
> We learn to teach by teaching—
> We learn to speak by speaking—
> We learn to typewrite by typewriting—
> We learn bookkeeping by keeping books—
> We learn business by carrying on business—
> We learn to play on a musical instrument by playing on it—
> We learn to cook by cooking—
> We learn to skate by skating—
> We learn law by the practice of law—
> We learn medicine by the practice of medicine—
> We learn to drive an automobile by driving one—
> We learn agriculture by farming.

How little does technical knowledge avail us in all these achievements.

We learn religion by doing the will of God.

We come to know Jesus Christ as we practice

ORTHODOXY AND OBEDIENCE

his spirit of love and kindness and self-sacrifice and unselfish service.

The most common and fatal form of unbelief is not unbelief in God, in Jesus the divine Saviour, in the immortality of man, but unbelief in the practicability of the principles of Jesus Christ. We have too many Churchmen who do not believe that we can do as Jesus Christ commands us and endeavor to make reparation by substituting orthodoxy for obedience. Mr. Moody was accustomed to saying that some people are so much taken up with what they are saved from that they fail to realize what they are saved for. We are more willing to accept Jesus Christ as Saviour than we are to obey him as Lord. A careful writer calls attention to the fact that in the twenty-seven books of the New Testament the word "Saviour" occurs only twenty-four times, while the word "Lord" is found 675 times. Jesus emphasized his Lordship: "Ye call me Master and Lord: and ye say well; for so I am." "If any man serve me, let him follow me." "If a man love me, he will keep my Word."

"Not everyone that saith unto me, Lord, Lord, shall enter into the kingdom of heaven; but he that doeth the will of my Father which is in heaven."

"Inasmuch as ye have done it unto one of the

least of these my brethren, ye have done it unto me."

> "And so the Word had breath and wrought
> With human hands the creed of creeds,
> In loveliness of perfect deeds,
> More strong than all poetic thought."

II

Inevitable injury results from a failure to obey the words of Christ.

There results injury to the intellect. In the long run it is to become skeptical. The final solvent of doubt is not thinking, nor feeling, nor praying, but doing the will of God.

Jesus said: "If any man will do his will." The strict translation is, "If any man willeth to do his (the Father's) will, he shall know of the teaching." The organ of spiritual knowledge is not the cultured mind, but the obedient will. There are certain spiritual truths which we know to be true, because we have lived them into certainty.

"We know as much as we do," was the motto of St. Francis of Assisi.

If we obey the principles of Jesus, then, amid the perplexities of the faith, "Light shall arise out of darkness."

We cannot silence our doubts by thinking; we cannot find God by searching, but we can do his

ORTHODOXY AND OBEDIENCE

will and then we shall know his doctrine. We keep in his presence by doing his will. Obedience clears the mind. Psychology reaffirms this idea of Jesus.

"That which is unexpressed dies."

In the realm of mind and spirit, the more you give, the more you have.

A dull, lifeless sort of orthodoxy may and does exist without obedience, but the true illumination of the mind and a vital grip of spiritual realities come from doing the will of God.

> "No one could tell me where my soul might be:
> I searched for God, but God eluded me;
> I sought my brother out and found all three."

To fail to obey is to spoil the emotions. It is to fall into a passive sentimentalism. Balzac said: "It is a perilous thing to separate feeling from action, to have learned to feel rightly without acting rightly. Feeling is given to lead to action. If feeling be suffered to awake without passing into duty, the character becomes untrue."

Hamlet was written to show us how any soul will miss its best and truest self and how the life must suffer shipwreck when the passion for musing and meditation never allows the truth it knows or the emotion it feels in high moments to pass into action. Hamlet is the fascinating but pathetic illustration of how disastrous to the soul and to the world is the separation in the same man of the dreamer from the doer, the thinker from the worker, the man of meditation from the man of action.

It is easy for the highest mind to make thought and feeling ends in themselves.

> "And the native hue of resolution
> Is sicklied o'er with the pale cast of thought."

Men of this type do not do anything, because they always see two ways of doing it. They stand meditating at the crossroads. The connection between the motive power and the operative faculties is lost. The engine is fired up, but the machinery stands still. Every person at some time has known and felt enough truth to have saved him. But a man lives on truth only by doing it.

There are people who feel very sensitively for the poor, the ignorant, the suffering, and the sinning.

Thousands of people look upon an imaginary picture of guilt, wretchedness, and sorrow on the pages of fiction or the stage of a theater, and think they are very pious because they can weep. They weep copious tears over the imaginary sorrows of imaginary characters who never had an existence outside of a novelist's imagination and have no helpful concern for real living human beings of flesh and blood and nerves. It is all a sorry sentiment. The emotions are spoiled. The sensibilities become hardened through inactivity and disobedience. The finer impulses are aroused, and when not given expression, they die.

There are people who welter in a sea of sentimentalism and substitute well-wishing for well-doing. A lady once said to me: "I know there is one good thing about me—I am tender-hearted. I never sit down with my husband to a good dinner on Sunday—and he will tell you exactly what I am telling you—but that I say to him that I wish somebody else had some of this dinner, and I sometimes call their names. I never buy for myself a new hat—and my husband will tell you this is true—but I say to him that I wish some other lady—and I sometimes call her name—had one just as fine."

It is a mushy sentiment which loves everybody and everything in general and nobody and nothing in particular.

There are many who sail on a shoreless sea of sentimentalism and arrive nowhere.

In a weak way they wish everybody well, and sigh over the sorrows of the wide world, from naked savages of the jungles to the hardly less savage denizens of city slums.

But they take it out in well-wishing. Their kind sentimentalism soothes them into a deadly slumber.

Through a failure to practice the principles of Jesus, the will is weakened and the backbone of the personality is separated from the forehead.

In spite of what we know—and what we feel—we may fail through inertia of the will.

The development of spiritual character calls for continued exercise as in the development of the physical powers and senses. These physical faculties can only be cultivated by exercise.

Do as much of the will of God as is plain to you. Be true to the duty you know. Treat your fellow man as an immortal being. Live yourself as an immortal, and faith in immortality comes easy.

By obedience to Jesus Christ, religious doubt is removed.

Personal enmity is removed as you set your will in the direction of good toward your enemy. Speak to your enemy. Speak as well of him as you can. Pray for your enemy. Act out the opposite of your feeling and your feeling becomes transformed. This is in accordance with the Scriptural injunction, "If thine enemy hunger, feed him."

Greed is removed as you act against it. Do the generous thing that you do not want to do. Cut through the grain of your nature. Act out the impulses that belong to your best moods and your best moments.

Unfortunate emotional states are removed by active obedience. You can nurse your grief and brood over it, but how much better it is to minister to others in sorrow and forget your own grief. Bear the burden of another and you lighten your own burden. Comfort others in their sorrow and you lessen your own sorrow. It is a kind of spiritual arithmetic in which addition means subtraction. Mr. Bright, the famous Englishman, gives an account of a visit of Mr. Cobden. Mr. Bright says: "I was in the depth of grief, almost despair; for the light and sunshine of my home had been extinguished. All that was left on earth of my young wife, except the memory of a saintly life and of a too brief happiness, was lying still and cold in the room above. Mr. Cobden called and, after expressing words of condolence, said: 'There are thousands of homes in England at this moment where wives, mothers, and children are dying of hunger. Now when the first paroxysm of your grief is past, I would advise you to come with me and we will never rest until the Corn law is repealed!'" The result of this partnership was felt by thousands of the grateful poor over England.

You are to dispel from the spirit the two dark demons of grouchiness and gloom, by active obedience. "If ye know these things, happy are ye if ye do them."

Act, if necessity calls for it, against the feeling. Carry out the agreeable and pleasant part. If you see an enemy, cross the street to shake hands with him—no, that will not be necessary, as you always meet him on the same side of the street.

Do the hard thing you are afraid to do and learn how to go will-foremost in doing the will of God.

III

Complaint is made that the ideals of Jesus are expressed in words that are visionary and impossible. The messages of Jesus are clothed in the language of the Orient, which is always highly figurative and symbolical. Figures of speech flourish with great luxuriousness in the East, and it is necessary to distinguish between literal and metaphorical expressions. Jesus spoke many words which he did not intend for a moment to be taken literally.

The Western people are painfully prosaic and literal and are prone to misunderstand the words of Jesus. Jesus dealt in principles, not in minute rules and precepts.

In his teaching "primal duties shine aloft as stars," but they are embodied in principles which are adaptable to all the changes in social, industrial, and political life. The literalist turns into an absurdity the words of Jesus. "But I tell you, you are not to resist an injury; whoever strikes you on the right cheek, turn the other to him as well. Whoever wants to sue you for your shirt, let him have your coat as well; whoever forces you to go one mile, go two miles with him; give to the man who begs from you, and turn not away from him who wants to borrow."

A sane interpretation determines what Jesus meant and discovers principles which the individual and society must practice for their own safety. His words proclaim principles of eternal value which we must proclaim and apply to life.

1. Love knows no limit except the limit which love itself imposes. Life is to be guided by love, and love will not allow that which is not best for the other life. To allow some ruffian to strike you on one cheek and then turn the other would be to encourage brutality. Jesus is certainly the best interpreter of his own words, and when smitten on one cheek did not turn the other. St. Paul, when struck on one cheek, did not turn the other.

It violates the principle of love to give to an able-bodied beggar, because it increases his laziness. Your giving is not withheld through selfishness, but because it would not be best for the other man.

2. Do not give place to private revenge. Do not indulge in retaliation. Do not allow your resistance to be prompted by malice. But you have no right to give encouragement to wrongdoing. If you tolerate physical violence and fail to protect the rights of property, you encourage the wrongdoer to inflict injustice on someone else. There could be justifiable resistance even to the point of killing another man in self-defense.

The right to life carries with it the right to protect your life against the man who would deprive you of life.

3. Be patient and forbearing under injuries. Retain your self-control. It will only hurt you to fly into a rage and act hastily. People who have little scruple in doing a wrong become enraged and violent when called upon to suffer wrong. It is better to suffer wrong than to do wrong. This principle runs through all the teachings of Jesus.

4. Do not show disrespect to public authority. Government is ordained of God. At times revolution has been necessary to overthrow government, but it is to be the last desperate resort.

5. The spirit of liberty is better than the force of coercion. Go the second mile willingly. Rise above law into the liberty of love. Let the sense of obligation rise to the glory of privilege. Let

ORTHODOXY AND OBEDIENCE

the freedom of service take the place of continued constraint.

6. Think more of what you may do for others than of what others may do for you. The note that runs through all the teachings of Jesus is, think more of your duties than of your rights.

Some think of the service others owe them; others think of the service they owe other people. This difference is as wide as the difference between selfishness and unselfishness, as wide as the difference between misery and happiness.

The people who lay the stress on their rights are very sensitive, contentious, continually aroused over some offense, real or imaginary, and are therefore unhappy. The people who lay the stress on their duties and the service they may render to others have no time nor disposition to become offended.

As they study how to be useful, happiness invariably comes as a by-product.

These are the principles of Jesus by which men really live.

Jesus gave to the world permanent principles by which men are to live rather than precepts which are applicable only to a particular situation. Society has moved from the simple to the complex since his day, but through all the centuries the principles of Jesus have proved sufficient for each particular age. In this day, with its intricate social, industrial, and political relationships, the principles of Jesus are practicable and applicable in the solution of our problems. All our modern discoveries and inventions, all our marvelous increase in all the realms of knowledge, all our unprecedented wealth, all our pressing social problems have only served to accentuate the timelessness of the principles of Jesus Christ.

CHAPTER VII

ORTHODOXY AND OBEDIENCE (Concluded)

The goal of the gospel of Jesus Christ involves both the perfection of the individual and the perfection of society. The undue emphasis upon a half-truth prevents the proclamation of the full gospel. The principles of Jesus cannot be dissolved into a thin humanitarianism nor narrowed into a strict individualism.

I

There are false theories which narrow the range of obedience to the principles of Jesus Christ, perverted notions which cripple and hurt life and hinder progress. There belong to individualism in religion certain elements which become evil only as they become excessive.

"The worst is the corruption of the best."

1. There is the form of orthodoxy which is rigid and unyielding and which does not hold, with the Puritan pastor, that "New light is to break forth continually from the Word of God." This kind of orthodoxy is frequently taken as a substitute for real Christian service.

The priest and Levite were engaged in their orthodox religious program, and did not find in their scheme of orthodoxy any requirement to turn aside and help a wounded man. It is a curious psychological fact that the intolerant doctrinaire is nearly always cruel. Another has said: "Zeal for doctrine can make a devil of a man as truly as zeal for rum-running—and no amount of church-going or money-contributing can atone for killing a woman's child with tuberculosis for the rents of an unsanitary tenement or giving it the rickets with adulterated foodstuffs."

The assumption of extraordinary piety and doctrinal soundness should certainly be accompanied by a Christian spirit. No man possesses a vital faith in Jesus Christ unless he is true to the Spirit of Jesus Christ. It should go without saying that we must all strive to be orthodox according to the real significance of the word. We should give no encouragement to an indefinite faith or a senseless warfare against creeds. But some things are to be remembered. First, your supposed orthodoxy may be at wide variance from the correct opinion. Second, if our orthodoxy were entirely true, there is no saving power in correct opinion.

A writer makes the quotation, "It is impossible to imagine that the devil has any erroneous opinions." When we inquire for the author of the expression we find that he is no less a personage than John Wesley. "The devils believe and tremble." There are some people who fall below this: they believe and do not tremble. Their orthodoxy falls below that of the devil in correctness of opinion, but they share his cruelty in holding to an orthodoxy without brotherliness and a religion without love.

Nothing has ever been so cruel in all history as religion without love. It resulted in the cruel massacres on the Eve of St. Bartholomew. The orthodox Church threatened to burn the miserable heretics who claimed that the earth moved around the sun. The Arminianism of the Methodists was a deadly heresy. Fitchett, in his life of Wesley, tells of an old Calvinistic minister to whom one said, "Would you not cut the throat of every Methodist you could find?" The old man blazed with fury, "And indeed did not Samuel hew Agag in pieces before the Lord?"

Back of this were the terribly orthodox Judaizers who hounded St. Paul to his death, and back of this was the orthodox Jewish Church that nailed Jesus Christ to the cross.

> "By the light of burning heretics
> Christ's bleeding feet we track,
> Toiling up new Calvaries ever,
> With the cross that turns not back."

There is the outcropping in our day of the same old spirit of persecution which, if it could, would use physical torture. Let us earnestly strive for real orthodoxy and at the same time beware of a so-called orthodoxy which is without the milk of human kindness.

To revert to a question that has been raised, what is the explanation of that cruel element in the religion of some people that leads to the exclamation, "O religion, what crimes are committed in thy name?"

It may be said by way of some extenuation that these cruelly religious people are striving in a mistaken way to preserve what they believe to be elements of value.

Again there is a fear which becomes frantic and easily passes into hatred.

Again there is an irritation which springs from the unconfessed suspicion of the weakness of their position which leads these religious people into a violent antagonism against all who do not pronounce their shibboleths, and an antagonism which manifests itself in general accusations, which is willing to dispense with all reason and argument.

Our only safety to-day is in the apostolic injunction, "Prove all things; hold fast that which is good."

2. There is the abiding peril of ecclesiasticism which is closely connected with the foregoing.

The Church is a divine institution and an indispensable factor in human society, but when

ORTHODOXY AND OBEDIENCE 151

it becomes an end in itself it is a harmful ecclesiasticism. It then loses sight of men in a system and is occupied with ecclesiastical machinery.

Every departure from established ecclesiasticism has come through a vision of wider service for men. By love alone does the Church justify her existence, a love that has the note of suffering in a compassionate search for the lost, and a note of joy when the lost are found. The one sin that received the brunt of the rebuke of Jesus was the sin of inhumanity.

His fierce condemnation of the Pharisees was for their inhumanity. The essence of sin is lovelessness. There are the Churchmen who place first humanity and the truth, and the Churchmen who place first ecclesiasticism and tradition. These are two continuing types.

The prophet stands first of all for the truth. The priest stands first of all for the institution. The prophet would modify the institution to harmonize with the truth. The priest would modify the truth to harmonize with the institution. The prophet with his primary devotion to the truth would save both the truth and the institution. The priest with his primary devotion to the institution would destroy both the truth and the institution. To follow the prophet is to preserve the institution which he loves. To follow the priest is to destroy the institution which he idolizes. There is the continued conflict between ideas and institutions. Thought refuses to be stationary; and when institutions refuse to change, war is the consequence.

There is no question as to which will win out in the long run.

A feature of lifeless ecclesiasticism is sacramental and ritualistic observances which narrow the range of obedience by being made a substitute for a helpful ministry to one's fellow man. This, according to the prophet Isaiah, is to turn "the solemn meeting into iniquity." This, according to Jesus Christ, is to neglect "the weightier matters of the law, judgment, mercy, and faith."

Another element in the peril of ecclesiasticism is the false dualism of the sacred and secular, which ignores a wide range of duties outside the so-called sacred.

An emphasis is given to the sacred by creating in contrast a whole realm of the secular in which the principles of Jesus are not supposed to be applicable. This is to make common and unclean that which God has sanctified. An individualistic philosophy turns industry and business into a selfish realm, where it is supposed that the Sermon on the Mount was never intended for application, and gives rise to the mottoes, "Don't mix business with religion" and "Business is business."

3. There is the religious mysticism, where the

worshiper shuts himself off from the human in rapt contemplation of the divine. This religious temperament is cultivated in the atmosphere of asceticism. Dr. F. G. Peabody writes: "The defect of mysticism is not its emotional exaltation, but its emotional isolation." In our exceedingly practical age we are in sore need of the cultivation of mystical fellowship and communion with God. We need to restore the lost art of meditation. A measure of mysticism could well replace much of our fussy activity. Mysticism is only harmful when the mystic endeavors to become so absorbed in God as to forget his mission to human society.

Much of this exaggerated individualism can be traced to an individualistic interpretation of the Scriptures, based on the allegorical or spiritualizing method which was much in vogue a generation ago. The social revolt of the Israelites against their oppressors in Egypt was turned into a picture of the escape of the individual soul from the Egypt of his sinful bondage into the promised land of Canaan. In the Parable of the Good Samaritan, as related by Jesus, the man who fell among thieves is a type of the human soul. The thieves are the devil and his angels, while Jesus is the Good Samaritan who commits the rescued soul to the Church to be cared for until his second advent.

This was a very comforting interpretation to

the individual who did not care to be disturbed over the misfortunes of his neighbor.

With all that may be reasonably and Scripturally urged against the false individualism of life, we are not to lose sight of the primary importance of life's individuality.

When Jesus came he put one life against the world: "What shall it profit a man, if he shall gain the whole world, and lose his own soul?" He tells us that the good shepherd will leave the ninety and nine and seek for the one lost sheep, and that there is joy in heaven over one sinner that is saved. He tells us in effect that which is so hard for some people to believe, that man was not made for the Sabbath, for the Church, for the State, but that the Sabbath and the Church and the State were made for man. He places the authority of the renewed individual life against traditions, customs, precedents, and external rules.

The reconciliation of the individual and social idea is to be sought. Society has witnessed hurtful extremes. The French Revolution, growing out of the excessive individualism of Rousseau, shattered society into atoms. At the other extreme is China with her ancestral worship, India with her caste system, Egypt with her priestly class, pressing down all individual peculiarity and power, and these civilizations were unable to stand. The same contrast is

ORTHODOXY AND OBEDIENCE

found in the Church. It was the aim of the Roman Catholic Church to solidify the world and the Church into a hard and fast uniformity, and ring the death knell of the individual. The dynamite which blew up this false solidarity was the religious experience of Martin Luther when he arose from his knees and exclaimed, "The just shall live by faith." Whatever in the Church or State tends to dwarf the individual is at enmity with the highest social order.

If the individual is not developed to the highest and to the utmost, he can never render the best social service. The ideal solidarity can only be constructed out of ideal individuals. You cannot build a marble palace out of mud. Faith creates two intuitions: that of liberty by which the soul possesses and asserts itself, and that of love by which the soul gives itself to others and enters into communion with them. True individuality is saved from anarchy and made social by love and sympathy. We see how the individual and social idea are perfectly correlated in the fullness of revelation. Baptism is individual. The Lord's Supper is social. In the great commandment love to God is individual, love to man is social. St. John stresses eternal life, which is individual, and the Synoptists the kingdom, which is social. In the first chapter of the last book of the Bible the perfect individuality is revealed when we are all kings and priests unto God, and in the last chapter of this last book the perfect social life is found in the ideal city of God.

Jesus Christ manifests his divine wisdom when he tells us in substance that when we make the most of the individual, then we can make the best of society.

To fail in the highest spiritual development of the individual is to lay the ax at the root of the tree of the highest social service.

You cannot construct an ideal social order out of sorry individuals. We are not to be obsessed by the high-sounding pretensions of an unspiritual humanitarianism which is only walking on feet of clay.

II

The demand of the principles of Jesus has to do both with personal salvation and with the spiritual and social welfare of other people. The first question, "What must I do to be saved?" must be followed by, "What can I do to save others?"

Bishop Gore of Oxford said: "I have constantly sat down bewildered before the blank and, it seems to me, simply stupid refusal of the mass of Church people to recognize their social duties. Why on earth is it? What produces this strange blindness of heart and mind? Often have I tortured my mind trying to find an answer to those questions, and tortured it in vain."

We find an explanation in the words of Dr. W. A. Brown: "In nineteenth-century Protestantism there grew up a conception of Christtianity, in principle largely self-centered and individualistic. The energies of Christians found sufficient outlet in the preparation of the individual for life after death, and the winning of new candidates for the citizenship of the future kingdom. Not transformation of the world, but escape from it, became the Christian message; not social leadership, but protest, the function of the Church."

There are two sets of qualities which belong to Christ's ideal of character and life which stand in contrast, but which should not be separated. They may be described on the one hand as the self-regarding qualities and on the other as the outgoing qualities. The self-regarding qualities refer to personal morals, such as honesty, temperance, truthfulness, and chastity. The outgoing qualities are Christian love, service, and self-sacrifice. The requirement of personal morals is assumed, of course, as of absolute necessity. Jesus placed emphasis on the outgoing qualities which men are prone to overlook. This marks the decided difference between the righteousness of Christ and the ordinary conception of righteousness. There are Church people who congratulate themselves on being without reproach in personal morals. But if we fail in these outgoing qualities we cannot win the approval of Jesus, however correct our private morals may be.

Many of the people whom Jesus condemned in scathing terms for their meanness, their unkindness, and their selfishness were people whose private morals were above reproach. There are women who in personal morals are as chaste as the snow on the mountain summit, but who are cold and unfeeling and unhelpful. A large number of Church people to-day are devoid of any sense of social responsibility. They go the round of their ceremonies and small activities with a complacency which ignores the fact that thousands of adults and thousands of children are, in practical effect, spiritually doomed by their physical wretchedness. A small portion of the professing Christian people, with the outgoing qualities of love, self-sacrifice, and service, with the wealth in their possession, with the scientific knowledge and agencies available, could bring a new hope and a new life to multitudes of starved and stunted lives.

How often we act as though unselfishness and sacrifice were only a sort of extra adornment of Christian character instead of being the very warp and woof of it.

ORTHODOXY AND OBEDIENCE 159

There is a wide gulf between our easy-going attitude and the passion with which Jesus taught and lived the law of self-sacrifice. The Church is entirely right in her insistence upon personal morals, and needs to be more insistent. But the widest departure from the leadership of Jesus Christ is our failure to live and stress these vital outgoing and permeative qualities of the Spirit of Christ.

Obedience to Jesus Christ has a far more searching application than many of us have been accustomed to think. Are we able to stand the test?

"Whosoever heareth these sayings of mine, and doeth them, I will liken him unto a wise man, who built his house upon a rock: and the rain descended, and the floods came, and the winds blew, and beat upon that house; and it fell not: for it was founded upon a rock. And everyone who heareth these sayings of mine, and doeth them not, shall be likened unto a foolish man, who built his house upon the sand: and the rain descended, and the floods came, and the winds blew, and beat upon that house; and it fell: and great was the fall of it."

We are fond of berating for his folly the man who in a theoretical unbelief denies the divine authority of Jesus. Jesus calls that man foolish who in practical unbelief ignores his authority. The condemnation of Jesus rests upon orthodoxy without obedience. "Not every one that saith unto me, Lord, Lord, shall enter into the kingdom of heaven; but he that doeth the will of my Father which is in heaven."

The worst foe to the Christian faith is practical infidelity. Christian people must dare to practice the principles of Jesus. Then we shall have the reign of love, then the lion and the lamb will lie down together, and the lamb will not be inside the lion.

Dr. Joseph A. Vance writes: "Then the landlord will befriend his tenant instead of fleece him. Then the theologian will contend earnestly for the faith once delivered to the saints, but he will contend like a saint and not like the devil. Then the clothing manufacturer will turn his sweatshop workers into a happy family—'the sucking child will play on the hole of the asp.' Then Christ will get his chance to show what he can do to heal the hurt of this poor old world; for men will no longer cloak cruelty under his name, but practice brotherly kindness. For then religion will be more than a flawless creed and a beautiful ritual; it will be a life, a life that takes its spiritual ideal not from public opinion, but from Jesus himself; and then that life, the only light of men, will get a chance to 'light every man that cometh into the world.'"

Bishop W. F. McDowell says: "For my part, I have no question as to one of the deadliest

ORTHODOXY AND OBEDIENCE

doubts prevalent in our time. It is the doubt as to the practicability and possibility of life at Christ's level. We are eager to be active and useful, bound to be orthodox if it takes all the shibboleths that can be quoted. We are strong on historic Christianity and weak on practical Christianity. We loudly assert the deity of Christ as a doctrine and then go on with perfectly ordinary, conventional emotions, decisions, and lives.''

III

Where shall we find the motive power that shall make us strong for the obedience which Christ requires? How shall power come into our frail lives which shall enable us to practice the principles of Jesus?

There is the threefold motive power, for my own sake, for the sake of other people, and for the sake of Jesus Christ—and these three are one, for the dynamic spirit of Jesus belongs to all these motives.

1. I should identify myself with Christ in his ministry to men for my own sake. In Christ I find the unity of my own life. The mark of the unchristian life is that life is divided and its different forces are in conflict. Life can only be at its best when it is unanimous. In obedience to Christ the conflict will cease between the will

and affections, between conscience and conduct, between the desires and aspirations and the thoughts and feelings.

In obedience to Christ, you enter into a blessedness of life. The blessedness of life follows the wholeness of purpose, "For me to live is Christ."

The perfection of life is to be found in obedience to Christ. "Ye are complete in him."

I owe it to myself not only to unify life, not only to add blessedness to life, not only to complete life, but to give continuance to my life. It has long been a matter of controversy as to whether the human soul is inherently immortal or conditionally immortal.

Whatever may be said of immortality of existence, we are confident that immortality of life is conditional. We shall enter into eternal life only as we live a life in obedience to Christ that is worth perpetuating, only as we live the eternal life here and now.

After all, why should I wish to continue a life unless it is worth continuing? Why should there be an idle wish to perpetuate a life that is not worth prolonging? Why should any man wish the perpetuation of his life through all eternity, when it is not even worth perpetuating here? If you have nothing to do but kill time here, how about the wholesale murder of killing an eternity of time? There are people who do not know how to fill a day with useful service. Will you then offer them the rolling ages without end?

It is only in Christ that we live a life which is worthy of being immortal.

2. I am to live in obedience to the principles of Jesus for the sake of other people.

There are the wide wastes of human woe and wretchedness which need relief. There is the need of enlightenment for the darkness of ignorance. There is the deepest of all human needs, the need of man as a sinner for the Saviour whom you are to make known to Him. The Christian life is to be as salt, purifying and preventing the spread of corruption. The Christian life is light shining in a dark place, a light which men most need in the darkness of sin and sorrow.

George Campbell, one of the greatest of Christian men, who devoted his life largely to the work of temperance reform, once administered the severest rebuke on a public platform. An avowed atheist, who had spoken before him in the interest of temperance, appealed to the strength of the human will as being sufficient for overcoming the appetitie for drink and referred to the uselessness of any aid outside a man's will. In a contemptuous side remark he said: "The man who invented gas has done more for the human race than all the preachers of Christianity." When Campbell arose to address the meeting he said: "I have been interested to hear my friend's opinion of what benefits humanity. If to-morrow I should be plunged into sorrow, or should find myself approaching the end of this brief life, I would desire some preacher of the Cross to tell me again its story for my comfort and strength. I suppose that my friend under similar circumstances would send for the gas-fitter."

In the midst of a sinning world, your life is to show the possibility and reality of victory through Jesus Christ over evil without and within. In the midst of a suffering world your life is to show to men the comfort of Christ's words, "Let not your heart be troubled." In the midst of a world that is mad for greed of gain, your life is to show to men the unselfish spirit of Christ and a supreme valuation for humanity and the things that are eternal. In the midst of a world that is amusement crazy, feeding on sensations and novelties, your life is to show to men the contentment which comes from the hidden wealth of the Spirit. In the midst of a world that is lawless and disobedient, you are to show to men the power of self-control and the glory of the obedient life. In the midst of a world with its bitterness and enmity, you are to show to men that "Love which beareth all things, hopeth all things, and endureth all things."

In the midst of a world with its selfish ambitions and thirst for human praise, you are to show to men the meekness and lowliness of spirit which seeks the commendation of God. In the midst of a world that has lost its way, you are to reflect the light of Him who is the Light of the World.

In the midst of a discouraged world you are to show the invincible hopefulness of life. In the midst of a world with its restlessness and tempest-tossed confusion, you are to show to men the restfulness, the serenity, the peace, and the joy which Jesus left as our inheritance.

In the midst of a world where so many are bruised and broken by the brutal forces of selfishness, where multitudes of children are not so much born as doomed into the world, you are to be the champions of a new social order that will give an opportunity to the submerged among us who have not the ghost of a chance in life.

In the midst of a world where the weak are the victims of the oppression of the strong, we are to interpret our own life's mission in terms of the life mission of Jesus himself.

"The Spirit of the Lord is upon me;
  Because he anointed me to preach good tidings to the poor;
  He hath sent me to proclaim release to the captives,
  And recovering of sight to the blind;
  To set at liberty them that are bruised,
  To proclaim the acceptable year of the Lord.''

It is only through obedience to Christ that

your life can bring this strength to the weakness of the world.

Is it not worth being a Christian to be able even in a measure to give forth a radioactive energy like this?

It is only through Christ that we can bring most help to men. There must be the upward look and the downward reach.

> "O strengthen me that while I stand,
>   Firm on the rock and strong in Thee,
> I may stretch out a loving hand
>   To wrestlers with the troubled sea."

3. I am to live in obedience to the principles of Jesus Christ for his own sake. This is the motive which permeates and elevates the other motives.

"He loved me and gave himself for me."

"The love of Christ constrains us."

"If a man love me, he will keep my words."

"We love him, because he first loved us."

"But for Christ's sake I have learned to count my former gains a loss; indeed I count anything a loss compared to the supreme value of knowing Jesus Christ my Lord. For his sake I have lost everything. I count it all the veriest refuse, in order to gain Christ."

In the State of New York a few years ago a young girl, Susie Parker, heard the call of God to give herself to missionary work in China, under the administration of Hudson Taylor. At the farewell meeting the father spoke of his daughter and her going away, closing with the words, "All I can say is, I have nothing too precious for Jesus." After the work of a few months, in which many were won to Jesus Christ, Susie Parker fell a victim to typhoid fever. In reply to a letter from Hudson Taylor telling of her useful life and triumphant death, the father wrote: "In the midst of my heartbreaking grief and desolation, I can only repeat what I said when my daughter went away, 'I have nothing too precious for Jesus.'"

There is no more pathetic and sublime picture in all the history of saintly lives than that of Mrs. Judson standing in the doorway of her home by the sea in Burma, watching the ship sail away that was carrying her children to America for their education. The long-dreaded hour had come. She must be separated for many years, if not for life, from her children, to stand by her husband in his work.

With many long and tender farewells she had bidden them good-by, and the great steamer had turned her prow to the open sea. The almost broken-hearted mother stood and watched the vessel until, through the mist in her eyes, it had ceased to be even a speck on the distant horizon, and then, turning into her room, she sank into a chair and exclaimed: "All this I do for the sake of my Lord."

A missionary gives us a chapter out of his experience:

When I was serving in India as a medical missionary a great epidemic of smallpox broke out and all the "white people" fled; but because my wife and I both were immune we remained, ministering to the sick and dying thousands.

One morning as I walked toward the village from our little residence I found in the path the most awful looking thing in the way of humanity that I have ever seen. He was in the last stages of that fearful disease; but because he was still alive, and for fear lest some beast of burden would trample him, I carried him out of the way and poured some water from a near-by stream into the foul mouth and went my way. That evening, as I returned, I found the rotting thing was still alive; and when on the morrow it still lived, I made a little broth and brought emollients and it lived.

At last it opened its eyes and I saw that the sight had not been destroyed, so I gave it food and "it" again became a living man. A few mornings later, as I came with some fruit and food, he was gone—gone without a "Thank you," and I returned discouraged to my wife and said: "He left without one word of gratitude, and he was nearer death than any man I ever saw." She replied: "We did not come out here for thanks, but for souls."

Eighteen months went by and India, freed from her epidemic, was gorgeous in her livery of green. Health and happiness had returned, as far as it was possible there, when one morning there strode into the residence a swarthy giant whose pockmarked body shone with sweat in the morning sun. Over his shoulder was the most beautiful elephant tusk ever seen in that part of India, while by his side hung a little leathern bag of Himalayan gold. He laid them at my feet and said, "I go get more."

My heart was touched and I said to him: "I did not do what I did for you in the hope of a reward."

"Then why did you do it?"

"I did it for Jesus' sake, for the sake of my Saviour, and yours, who came from Heaven and lived and died that we might be saved from our sins and have peace and joy in our hearts."

His giant body trembled and, dropping on his knees at my feet, he cried: "O white man, white man, show me HIM—Show me HIM."

No vague sense of human brotherhood, no soft sentiment of humanitarianism can put the spiritual morale into a man's heart for a service like this. It is only the motive that springs from a response to the love of Jesus Christ for us that can maintain us on the high level of heroic and self-forgetful service. We shall respond to the urgent call of Christ to grapple with the pressing duties, when the need of humanity is greatest, where the night of human wretchedness is darkest, where the wild waves of human woe are most relentless, only as we draw the strength of our motive power from Christ who is our Lord and our Saviour.

A young college student was persuaded by his mother to visit an art gallery where a fine painting, "The Man of Galilee," was being shown. The young man had no artistic taste and was not much interested in the gallery. After gazing at the picture for some moments with intense earnestness, he started to go out, when one of the attendants, who noticed his earnest attitude, said to him: "It is a great picture." "Yes, it is a great picture," replied the boy. "And it is well named, 'The Man of Galilee.'" Then the student went back and looked at it again—gazed upon that face until his gaze be-

came transfixed, and with softened voice he said:
"O thou Man of Galilee, if there is anything
I can do to help you in the work that you are
doing in the world, count on me, count on me."
O, may we all, as we look up into the face of our
Christ, say it, say it as we have never said it
before: "Count on me—count on me."

>"I said, 'Let me walk in the fields.'
>   He said, 'No, walk in the town,'
> I said, 'There are no flowers there.'
>   He said, 'No flowers, but a crown.'
>
> I said, 'But the skies are black;
>   There is nothing but noise and din.'
> And He wept as he sent me back;
>   'There is more,' he said; 'there is sin.'
>
> I said, 'But the air is thick,
>   And fogs are veiling the sun.'
> He answered, 'Yet souls are sick,
>   And souls in the dark undone .'
>
> I said, 'I shall miss the light,
>   And friends will miss me, they say.'
> He answered, 'Choose to-night,
>   If *I* am to miss you, or they.'
>
> I pleaded for time to be given.
>   He said, 'Is it hard to decide?
> It will not seem hard in heaven
>   To have followed the steps of your Guide.'
>
> I cast one look at the fields,
>   Then set my face to the town;
> He said, 'My child, do you yield?
>   Will you leave the flowers for the crown?'

Then into His hand went mine,
  And into my heart came He;
And I walk in a light divine
  The path I had feared to see."

CHAPTER VIII

SOCIAL SOLIDARITY

The interrelationship, interconnection, and interdependence of the varied elements and forces of the universe are verified by numerous examples.

> "Nothing in this world is single;
> All things by a law divine
> In each other's being mingle."

> "There's a part of the sun in an apple
> There's a part of the moon in a rose,
> There's a part of the flaming Pleiades
> In every leaf that grows."

The lowliest of things is related to and ministers to the whole moving scheme.

The bacteria remove deceased organisms and make life possible in the world. They fix nitrogen, so that it is possible that the farmer of the future, instead of the present cumbersome method in the fertilization of the soil, with a small tube of colorless liquid will inoculate the soil.

There are from 50,000 to 500,000 earthworms in one acre of land and they pass multiplied tons of soil through their bodies and increase the productiveness.

The birds destroy destructive insects and protect trees and fruits. If deprived of birds, the earth would soon become uninhabitable.

The flower is so related to the entire universe that if we understood the flower we would understand the sun 90,000,000 miles away.

> "Flower in the crannied wall,
> I pluck you out of the crannies,
> Hold you here, root and all, in my hand,
> Little flower—but if I could understand
> What you are, root and all, and all in all,
> I should know what God and man is."

In order to collect enough nectar to make one pound of honey industrious bees must go from hive to flower and back again 2,750,000 times. Then, when you think how far these bees sometimes fly in search of these clover fields, often one or two miles distant from the hive, you will begin to get a small idea of the number of miles one of the industrious little creatures must travel in order that you may have a pound of honey.

The relation of cats to a crop of red clover sounds rather remote. But bees fertilize the clover, the field mice destroy the bees, and the cats destroy the mice—so that the more cats there are, the fewer field mice, the more bees, and the more red clover. We may go still further. It is well known that unmarried ladies of a certain or uncertain age take special care of the cats, so that the more unmarried ladies you have, then the more cats, the fewer field mice, the more bees, and the more red clover. Of course, the fewer unmarried ladies you have, then the fewer cats, the more field mice, the fewer bees, and the less red clover.

Now it is a very probable supposition that certain sunspots turned toward the earth mean unfavorable weather conditions and a bad financial year.

It is a well-known statistical fact that a bad financial year means fewer marriages, and then certain sunspots would result in a larger number of unmarried ladies, and there would be more cats, fewer mice, more bees, and more red clover. This, however, would be on condition that the larger number of bees would help the red clover more than the bad weather would injure the clover.

There is no attempt to arrange in any logical order illustrations of the varied interconnections of things that appear unrelated.

We are prone to regard the dust as worse than useless. But it is the dust which gives us the blue of the sky and sea, the beauty of the dawn and the glory of the sunset, and the diffused daylight. Alfred Russel Wallace says: "It has recently been discovered that dust plays an important part in nature, a part so important that it is doubtful whether we could even live without it. To the presence of dust in the higher atmosphere we owe the formation of mists, clouds, and gentle, beneficial rains, instead of waterspouts and destructive torrents.''

The scientific student in his laboratory appears to have no contact with practical life. But Pasteur discovers the microörganisms that destroy the silk-worms and brings material prosperity to France. The chemist makes possible the steel industry. The scientist, with his discovery of anæsthetics and antiseptics, is very closely related to practical life.

A North Carolina presiding elder who was a close observer of country life connects Ford cars and eugenics. He says that Ford cars have widened the territory of young men and young women and enlarged the range of their matrimonial choice. In their former limited communities, there were more unfortunate marriages among those of blood kin, but now Ford cars have removed this handicap.

Thus the interconnection appears between Ford cars, good roads, and eugenics.

Again the value of money depends on the interrèlationship and interdependence of society.

What makes your money valuable? Suppose that everybody should die to-day and you should own the whole earth.

The seven ages of man as revised by someone are said to be: First age, sees the earth; second age, wants it; third age, hustles to get it; fourth age, decides to be satisfied with about one-half of it; fifth age, would be satisfied with less than half of it; sixth age, now content to possess a six-by-two strip; seventh age, gets the strip.

But suppose to-morrow you should own the earth, the lands and banks and railroads and skyscrapers—if you were alone, you would be poorer than the poorest tramp. It is society which gives value to your possessions.

Our lives are inextricably interwoven with the lives of others. This interconnection binds us with other lives of the past, the present, and the future.

Each man stands at the center of a vast network of ancestors. Looking back on the past, we see how intimately one life is bound up with millions of others. Even physically it has taken all the generations from the beginning of time to produce us, all the generations of men in their crossing and intermingling to make you and me. It is estimated that going no further back than the Norman conquest, each of us has 16,000,000 ancestors, from each of whom we have received some contribution of weakness or strength. We, in turn, shall leave some impress on millions of descendants. In a little while our

SOCIAL SOLIDARITY 177

brief lives will be rounded with a sleep, but what of the generations that follow who shall be made stronger or weaker by the kind of character which we possess?

Of more immediate application, however, are our varied relationships with our own generation. There is our interrelationship on the material side. The higher the stage of civilization, the more complex are the relationships of life. "We are members one of another." Ex-President Harris of Amherst College has drawn for us the details of one small area of a man's unescapable membership in human kind. "When he rises a sponge is placed in his hand by a Pacific Islander, a cake of soap by a Frenchman, a rough towel by a Turk. His merino underwear he takes from the hand of a Spaniard, his linen from a Belfast manufacturer, his outer garments from a Birmingham weaver, his scarf from a French silkgrower, his shoes from a Brazilian grazier. At breakfast his cup of coffee is poured by natives of Java and Arabia, his rolls are passed by a Kansas farmer, his beefsteak by a Texas ranchman, his orange by a Florida negro."

What is involved in what we eat, wear, spend, and use? It means the lone shepherd on the mountain side, the weary weaver at the loom, the weather-beaten sailor at the mast, the engineer driving through the storm, the miner in the depth of the earth, the fisherman on the foggy coast, the plowman in the furrow, and the cook in the drudgery of the kitchen.

Dr. Newell Dwight Hillis writes: "The new solidarity of commerce makes war foolish, and compels international arbitration. . . . By ten thousand cables and electric threads God is binding the nations together in weaving one warp and woof—a world people. Physically, Providence has distributed his gifts so that no nation is a complete nation. He gives wheat to the North, cotton to the South, tea and spices to the East, sugar and coffee to the tropics. No man is a full man, because of the distributed intellectual gifts. God took the ideal man and broke him up into fragmentary men, so that they would have to unite their gifts through brotherhood to produce a civilization just as God broke up the light and distributed it in fragmentary stars, and then bound the stars together into one cosmic system. He gives religion to the Hebrew, law to the Roman, culture to the Greek, the love of detail to the German, wit and beauty to the Frenchman, colonization to the Englishman, practical invention to the American, mental alertness to the Japanese, patience to the Chinese, endurance to the Russian. The zones have to exchange gifts. Insects flit from flower to flower, and make harvests possible. Steamships are commercial devices of God for fertilizing nations into flowers and fruit, carrying honey from

SOCIAL SOLIDARITY

one civic cup to another civic bloom. The world is the Father's house, and all men are brothers.''

The social and moral phase of our solidarity is freighted with the most portentous consequences.

We have become so obsessed with a strict individualism that we have ignored the fact that we belong to an indivisible whole, that social solidarity is the inescapable law of human life, and that if "one member suffer, all the members must suffer with it."

We have too largely ignored our social obligations through a miserable individualistic interpretation of life and salvation. We have been too much afraid of an abstract political theory of paternalism, but we have not been afraid to neglect living, suffering creatures of flesh and blood. As someone has forcefully said: "We do most of our thinking below our diaphragms." Much of our thinking has been predetermined by our self-interest. We are inclined to make ourselves comfortable in a smug orthodoxy which conceals from us our social solidarity, ignores our social obligation, and prevents the development of a social conscience.

"Is it well that while we range with science, glorying in the Time,
City children soak and blacken soul and sense in city slime?"

"There among the glooming alleys progress halts on palsied feet,

> Crime and hunger cast out maidens by the thousands on the street.
>
> There the master scrimps his haggard sempstress of her daily bread;
> There a single sordid attic holds the living and the dead.
>
> There the smolding fire of fever creeps across the rotted floor,
> And the crowded couch of incest in the warrens of the poor.''

The privileged class may not be willing to place even the tips of their dainty fingers beneath our social burden and they may neglect the bruised and broken, but these very weak ones, like another Samson, in the blindness of brute strength will tear away the very pillars of our civilization. We are all in the same boat and we are going to sail or sink together.

We shall lift up the submerged through the power of the gospel of Jesus Christ or their weight will drag us down. The privileged class of France supposed that they could shut themselves off in proud isolation from the unprivileged; but the red revolution was the negation of their folly, when the blood of French people ran redder than the purple clusters of French vineyards.

I repeat that we have been so prejudiced against any indication of paternalism, and so warped in our thinking by certain false ''orthodox'' interpretations, that we have allowed idiots to breed with all the prolificness that is charac-

SOCIAL SOLIDARITY 181

teristic of them, and have allowed children to rot in filth and immoral surroundings and grow up in ignorance, without any schools except the school of criminality, because we have proceeded under the dangerous delusion that parents have a divine right to do as they will with their own. You may leave these masses of wretchedness and festering sores of society alone, but they will not leave you alone. Has society no right to protect itself? Are we not yet wise enough to know that the fierce fires of retribution inevitably follow all of our selfish neglect? The human family is one and cannot be elevated in sections. No class can be independent of another class. There is the pride that desires separation, but isolation is impossible. You may ignore the "black bottom" of your cities and heed not if a neglected negro population live a living death in filth and sexual disease, but you can trace the terrible vengeance when you see the little white babies that are born blind and never see.

Dickens, the novelist of the poor, told us decades ago: "The poorest man has his revenge on the rich, for even the winds are his messengers, and every drop of his corrupted blood propagates infection and contagion somewhere. There is not a cubic inch of any pestilential gas on which he lives, not one obscenity or degradation about him, not one ignorance, nor a wickedness, nor a brutality of his committing, but shall work its retribution through every order of society up to the proudest of the proud, and the highest of the high."

As a further illustration of this social solidarity, Carlyle gives us the incident of the poor widow dying in neglect. "She took typhus fever and killed seventeen of you—very curious. The forlorn Irish widow applies to her fellow creatures as if saying, 'Behold I am sinking bare of help; ye must help me. I am your sister, bone of your bone; one God made us; ye must help me.' They answer: 'No; impossible; thou art no sister of ours.' But she proves her sisterhood; her typhus fever kills them; they actually were her brothers, though denying it. Had human creature ever to go lower for a proof?"

"If virtue is better than blackest of crime,
If sunlight is cleaner than foulest of slime,
Then they that are right must righten the wrong,
And the weak must be saved by the strength of the strong."

It is only as the strong save the weak that the strong themselves will be saved.

Dr. Josiah Strong writes: "Men are seeing more and more clearly that their interests are not individual and isolated, but common. First, men who were engaged in the same industry discover that their interests are really one, and they organize their unions; then men in different but interrelated industries see that they have much in common, and different unions combine; then men see the common interests of all labor, and there is a movement toward national federation; then they discover the necessity of international organization and action. Capital has been moving in the same direction. First, there was the partnership, then the corporation, then the combination of corporations in increasing numbers and magnitude, until there is developed at last a trust as broad as the continent. Capital and labor have not yet discovered that their interests are really one, that they must coöperate like the two wings of a bird; but that discovery will come in time, and then they will combine."

Thus we find an unmistakable current in the world of thought toward what might be called the consciousness of solidarity—something so new in kind or degree that it has compelled the use of a new word to express it, and we hear of the "solidarity of labor," the "solidarity of society," the "solidarity of the race."

III

So as we widen our conception we find that for better or for worse the whole world is bound together and interrelated.

It is supreme folly to talk of the United States retaining a splendid isolation. A League of

Nations in some effective form must be worked out or civilization will go down in the carnage and chaos of war. We have a number of politicians who were born out of due season, about five hundred years too late, and they have not yet found out that the world is a unit and that no member of this world organism can suffer without all the members suffering.

Carlyle wrote: "There is not a Red Indian hunting by Lake Winnipeg can quarrel with his squaw, but all the world will smart for it. Will not the price of beaver rise?" The world is so woven together by a variety of connecting ties that both ideas and diseases are highly contagious. Spanish influenza rapidly crosses national boundary lines and the theories of Russian Bolshevism are accepted by many American laborers. There are belated politicians who do not know the age in which we are living, who cannot "discern the signs of the times."

We have had quite enough chauvinism and jingoism. There must be developed the international mind.

The blackest blotch on American history is the policy of selfish isolation to which our country has been committed.

For many decades a wave of indignation and protest has swept over the nation at every report of Armenian massacres. But when the opportunity was given for America to assume the

SOCIAL SOLIDARITY

mandate over Armenia the political leaders took counsel of cowardly prudence.

America could have largely prevented the imminent perils that threaten the very perpetuity of more than one European nation. The United States forgot that she was a debtor to other nations. She followed the leadership of demagogues rather than duty. Our nation fell from the pinnacle of idealism into the slough of materialism. The very material motives which influenced our blind guides are proving to be against our material prosperity. Prosperous America cannot even continue prosperous by a policy of national aloofness. The world is so knit together and interrelated that no people can remain independent of what happens in the remotest part of the world. The appeal of commerce will at last penetrate thick-skinned sensibilities, where the appeal of conscience failed. In the meantime the work of rebuilding a wrecked world is arrested.

But America will be compelled to think in terms of world solidarity, even if she does her thinking "below the diaphragm."

IV

There is no clearer mark of the oneness of Jesus Christ with divinity than his conception of the oneness of humanity. St. Paul followed his Lord as the matchless exponent of the Christian ideal of the unity of the human race. "Man is renewed into knowledge after the image of him that created him; where there cannot be Greek and Jew, circumcision and uncircumcision, barbarian, Scythian, bondman, freeman; but Christ is all, and in all." "He made of one every nation of men for to dwell on the face of the earth."

Seneca, a contemporary of St. Paul and an outside saint, must have possessed the divine afflatus when he said: "We are members of a vast body. Nature made us kin when she produced us from the same things and to the same ends. I will look upon all lands as belonging to me, and my own land as belonging to all. I will so live as if I knew that I am born for others, and on this account I will give thanks to nature. She gave me alone to all men, and all men to me alone. I will know that the world is my country. Nature bids me assist men. Wherever a man is, there is room for doing good."

The world sympathy of Jesus Christ should certainly be the working principle of the Christian. Perhaps no man of his generation more forcefully expressed the mind of Christ and more sympathetically interpreted his ideal of world unity than Charles Cuthbert Hall:

"The genuineness of Christ's attitude, as representing not theory but conviction, is proved by his reverent treatment of humanity, by his world-consciousness in teaching, by his vision of purpose when advancing to a sacrificial death, and when sending, by means of apostolic messengers, to the uttermost bounds of the known earth, his gospel of a redeemed humanity.

"I can truly say that in intellectual and spiritual intercourse with certain Orientals, who by anthropologists would be classified under several different categories, I have felt that human kinship which scarcely may be described by a term less strong than consanguinity of the soul. The Churches of the West which have looked upon themselves proudly as the dispensers of this religion may have mastered its rudiments only. The mystery of God in Christ, which was hid from ages and generations until the incarnation of the Living Word was accomplished in the fullness of time, may contain inner glories as yet undreamed of—glories not accessible until the eager West consents to sit as a disciple at the feet of the ancient East, learning through the Oriental consciousness to search the deep things of God. One cannot divide East from West in the matter of religious interaction any more than in the matter of commercial interaction.

"It is not then wholly as the giver, but also as

the receiver, that the West is to approach the East bearing the gospel of Christ. She is not to say, 'This is the gospel which I know and which I teach you,' but rather: 'Here is the gospel which I know in part, according to the gifts and insight of the West. Share it with me, O soul of the Eastern world; help us to know better, through you, that gospel and that Christ.' "

Our human life will never be complete, our religious faith will never be complete, until each man possesses the wealth of all men and all men possess the wealth of each man.

In man's redemption lies the redemption of the whole world, and in the redemption of the whole world lies the complete redemption of men.

St. Paul rises to the sublime height of the conception of the solidarity of the entire creation. "For the earnest expectation of the creation waiteth for the revealing of the sons of God." "For the creation itself also shall be delivered from the bondage of corruption into the liberty of the glory of the children of God." Jesus Christ as the perfect man sprang "as a root out of dry ground," but perfect humanity can only grow out of the spiritual soil of a redeemed world.

Toward this goal has been set the aspiring and

striving soul of humanity through all the æons of its progress.

"Where is one that, born of woman, altogether can escape
From the lower world within him, moods of tiger or of ape?
Man as yet is being made, and ere the crowning age of ages,
Shall not æon after æon pass and touch him into shape?
All about him shadow still, but, while the races flower and fade,
Prophet-eyes may catch a glory slowly gaining on the shade,
Till the peoples all are one, and all their voices blend in choric
Hallelujah to the Maker: 'It is finished; man is made.' "

CHAPTER IX

THE NEW CRUSADE

The crusade of to-day is not one of romance or sentiment, like that which led the medieval Church to rescue the holy sepulcher of the risen Christ. It is a crusade whose daring aim is to bring the world of humanity under the reign of the risen Christ. As we gain some insight into the real antagonism and possible achievements of the present and future, we see the Captain of our Salvation leading in an eightfold crusade —the Crusade of Personal Evangelism, Christian Coöperation, Democracy, Social Betterment, National Welfare, Internationalism, World Peace, and the Kingdom of God on Earth.

I

There is the crusade of Personal Evangelism. We must never lose sight amid general movements of the high spiritual ministry of bringing the individual into the relationship of reconciliation with God and with his fellow men.

1. There is the reflex influence of personal

evangelism on the Church itself. It wins the respect of a community for the Church. The bootblack can tell you with amazing accuracy what the Church ought to do. The world knows that if the members of a Church are really doing the work of Christ they will be seeking the lost.

It changes the atmosphere of the average Church. Love is the supreme motive that carries the message. Bickerings, jealousies, quarrels, and petty prejudices cannot live in the Church. The spiritual temperature is raised. There is the unity of life and warmth, not the unity of frozen ice. It will vitalize the worship of the Church. The Church member who never does anything but listen and absorb will at last grow weary of listening.

There is the effect on the preacher himself. When the members give themselves to personal evangelism, his preaching catches a fervor that is a surprise even to himself.

The evangelism results in a sane emotional life. There are people who simply want their emotions stirred, as a matter of spiritual luxury, who are willing for a preacher to pour out nervous energy to stimulate their morbid sensibilities. If you will go out and live Christianity during the week and seek to save some one who knows not Christ, you will soon have all the emotions you need.

2. To win men to Jesus Christ is both to share

and increase your spiritual treasure. You must have before you can give. You must know before you can witness. You must possess something that is worth passing on. If you know Jesus Christ as one who saves you from sin and gives you strength and comfort, then you are in possession of something that every person without Jesus Christ needs. The sharing of spiritual treasure multiplies the treasure.

In material things, such as land and money, to give means a subtraction. But according to the arithmetic of heaven, to share a spiritual treasure means addition.

St. Paul makes a further application of gaining spiritual riches when he tells us that we may enter into a possession of human lives. "I seek not yours, but you." This is the instinct of property raised to its heavenly quality. We are not to fall into the common delusion of desiring what men have rather than men themselves. We have a real ownership in beautiful landscapes, in air and light and stars and mountains. Higher still a man enters into the heritage of men whom he has won to Christ. We have, as Horace Bushnell reminds us, a property right in every one we meet, if only we may bring to their lives a blessing. He says in one of his great sermons: "In this manner it is given us for our beautiful divine privilege to have a property in every one we meet, if only we can find how to bless them. Owning, we have a field where mines richer than those of gold are open to us on every side. Going after what men have, we get nothing; after men themselves, a property that is everlasting." If we go after fame, then how transient is the praise of man, "whose breath is in his nostrils." If we seek riches and the mere externalities of life, then we meet the statute of limitation: "We brought nothing into this world, and it is certain we can carry nothing out." All material properties are left behind. There is indeed no real estate, but spiritual property. Death only brings to perfect consummation this ownership.

II

The Crusade for Coöperation must supplant the philosophy and practice of extreme individualism.

Man alone is a very helpless being in the world. He becomes strong by relating himself to forces outside himself. Man relates himself to natural power in the world and by use of steam, electricity, and machinery multiplies his own power a thousandfold.

The religion of Jesus Christ is one of power. As we relate ourselves to him and believe on him, our own weakness becomes strength and our own power is multiplied.

1. Man must coöperate with man. Along with self-preservation, coöperation or comradeship is one of the strong instincts of the human. The small boy said: "Mother, I wish that I were two little puppies, so I could play together."

Even the huge, ferocious animals that were strictly individualistic have lost out while the forms of animal life that live in herds and hives continue.

The history of civilization is the history of coöperation. The individual Cyclops, however huge, was powerless against the feeblest band. The tribes that did not know how to coöperate were exterminated. The tribes that knew how to coöperate became a nation.

2. Coöperation is the test of intelligence. Some one said to the manager of an asylum, where there was a large number of insane people, "Are you not afraid they will combine against you?" He replied: "No. If they had sense enough to coöperate, they would not be here." The idiot (or "idiotes") was originally the private man who did not participate in public affairs. In the seventeenth century Jeremy Taylor said: "Humility is a duty in great ones, as well as in the idiots." The word comes to signify a rude, ignorant, unskilled person, who had not been developed by contact and coöperation with others. It then comes to have its present meaning of one who is seriously deficient in

intellect. The failure to coöperate does not always mean lack of intellect or character, but it does mean failure to put both of these to the best use.

3. The obstreperous individual may go on the assumption, "I am so much wiser than others that I cannot work with ordinary people."

Or the person may say in effect, "I am so perfect myself, I do not know how to work with imperfect people."

St. Paul tells us that the failure to coöperate is due to two contrasted dispositions.

First, there is self-depreciation. The foot complains because it is not the hand, the ear because it is not the eye. So men and women fail to be of any use in the Church because they think that they do not amount to anything.

Second, there is the depreciation of others. The head despises the feet. The eye thinks it has no need of the ear. The eye is such a fine creature that it is the aristocratic member of the body. But there are many things the eye cannot do. It must work with the other members of the body. So St. Paul says in substance that there are Church members who refuse to work with others because they do not feel good enough, and there are Church members who refuse to work with others for the reason that they feel too good.

4. We are not in the millennium, and perfect

coöperation is not to be expected, but it is a necessary condition of success and progress in both Church and State. He is a sorry citizen who says that the government of the country or city is not being run to suit him, and he will have nothing to do with it. He is a sorry Church member who says that the church is not being run to suit him, and he will have nothing to do with it. It is highly important to know how to give and take, work in a team, and play the game. The game of baseball might atone for some of its sins if it would teach the Church how to do teamwork. The Church would be excusable for attending the game in a body if the members would learn the lesson of the almost perfect coöperation of a baseball nine.

5. Strict individualism is intolerable and impossible. The law of society wisely overrides the obstreperous individual. Take, for example, a town which has reached a certain state of growth. The individualist says: "My property is my own, and I don't want a paved sidewalk. I can do as I please with my own. It is outrageous and unjust to intrude on my liberty." But the community says: "Why so hot, my little man? Try to cool off a little; it will be good for your health. You are not living in the midst of savagery, but in civilization. Try to catch up with the procession, and keep step. Remember, please, that it is the whole com-

munity that makes your little individual possession worth anything at all; and if you are not civilized enough to coöperate, we will make you coöperate."

Harry Emerson Fosdick writes: "The old age urges that all nations must be armed against each other; the new age replies that all nations must coöperate for the world's peace. In that choice between Christ and Satan, Christians have an enormous stake. War in its origin, motives, methods, and issues is the most powerful anti-Christian influence on earth. But individual service alone cannot handle the problem. The coöperative organization of all the international good will there is, is indispensable."

This is the truth of Kipling's lines:

"As the creeper that girdles the tree trunk the law runneth forward and back;
For the strength of the pack is the wolf, and the strength of the wolf is the pack."

It is the truth of the inspired word: "One shall chase a thousand, and two shall put ten thousand to flight." Two are far more than twice as strong as one.

Perfect coöperation can hardly be expected, since there are some individuals who are peculiarly constructed; but it is only as Christian people learn to play the game, do teamwork, and keep step that we shall accomplish the high tasks that are set before us.

It was teamwork which at last brought victory to the Allied forces in the World War.

> "It ain't the guns or armaments, nor the funds that they can pay,
> But the close coöperation that makes them win the day.
> It ain't the individual nor army as a whole,
> But the everlasting teamwork of every blooming soul."

6. It appears to the long-suffering public that the enormous waste from capital and labor conflicts bears every mark of stupidity. The general public is convinced that intelligent men ought to be able to come to an agreement that will prevent such heavy losses to the parties directly concerned as well as the people in general.

We have no sort of hesitancy in saying that we thoroughly believe in organized labor. The right of organized labor should be recognized as unreservedly as the right of organized capital. This right is not disputed to-day except by certain belated minds.

7. It is interesting to observe in what curious and commonplace ways the falseness of the old individualism is exposed. Some years ago I was in a section of Georgia where the live issue was the question of tick-eradication. I was informed that if the coöperation had been complete the tick would already have become an-tiq-uated. The farmers are confident that, despite the an-

THE NEW CRUSADE 199

tics of a few who howl for individual rights, the cattle will soon be free of this pest.

We are fully aware that this is a very ticklish subject, but it is entirely too serious to be tick-led over. We propose to ar-tic-ulate our remarks carefully, with the realization that we must be very par-tic-ular in what we say.

It is passing strange that illustrious political agitators have wildly ges-tic-ulated as anti-tick-eradicators. So the question entered poli-tics and has influenced the mind of the voter as he made out his tick-et. None of this strife would ever have risen if the tick had been as strict an individualist as the anti-tick-eradicator. But the tick possesses very neighborly qualities and insists on visiting. The tick, though not held in high esteem, breaks down the theory of individualism. Society is re-tic-ulate. Men and their interests are interrelated, so that coöperation is the common-sense law of life. The man who does not believe in coöperation should pack up, buy a tick-et, and move away from all human society.

Go to the tick, thou individualist; consider her ways, and be wise.

Professor Ellwood writes: "Coöperation is the inner constructive principle of group life; and the wider and more harmonious this coöperation is, the richer and the more perfect is the social life of mankind as a whole. Civilization and all its values, then, depend upon the continuance and development of coöperation among men. Obviously a social religion must aim to maximize coöperation, and it will be successful in doing this only as it teaches the value of mutual service."

8. The Christian Church, with its gospel of coöperation as against competition, may practice its own principle, when the wisdom of it has been justified in all the other realms of human service and activity. The reproach of Protestantism has been the weakening division as against the coöperative forces of unrighteousness.

A new spirit, however, is stirring within the mighty hosts of Protestant Christianity. We are waking to the folly of our more than two hundred competing and contending sects, and the subdivision has gone to such absurd extremes that some of these denominations are scarcely more than denominational insects. In numerous towns and communities we have a situation and attitude like that described in the report of a pastor of a certain denomination when he said: "My church is in a fearful condition. The members are indifferent and fail to support the Church. We are dependent on a missionary appropriation. The outlook is hopeless; but, thank the Lord, the other Churches are no better." The recognition of the fact is being forced upon us that we cannot cope with our immigrant problem, our race problem, our labor problem, our liquor problem, and our social problem unless there is a closer and more vital coöperation of Christian Churches.

The address of Dean Franklin N. Parker, of the Candler School of Theology, before the First General Council of the United Methodist, Presbyterian, and Congregational Churches of Canada will prove to be a notable and historic utterance: "It may be said that the new conception of the widening claims of social life, our responsibilities to men and women and children, and the vital and everlasting needs of the poor, the laborer, and the unprivileged class has compelled us to think more in the terms of humanity and less in the terms of formularies and symbols. And it is for organized Christianity to-day to gather around its Lord and Leader and in the might of the new crusade to pledge itself not merely to fidelity to the memory of a great creed, but a challenge to lead the world to do as Jesus did, to practice his imperishable ideals, and at whatever cost, and to make the nations see that the supreme message of the incarnation is reconciliation. As the great apostle to the Gentiles states: 'Now then we are ambassadors for Christ, as though God did beseech you by us; we pray you, be ye reconciled to God.' Of course, I am aware that in appealing to a passage of Scripture such as this some may challenge me, urging the fitness of a passage as applied only to the individual. But I cannot conceive that this is the only scope of the gospel message. I think that the very tendency to so limit it has stood in the way of the progress of the gospel for centuries.

Once more I am reminded that the passage in St. John where our Lord prays for unity refers to a spiritual unity, refers to spiritual unity alone, and has no relation to the Church's organic and visible order, but this has never seemed convincing to me. It must be true that Jesus Christ does make men one; and if humanity is humanity and man is man, it ought to affect profoundly and in a far-reaching way all organized life in whatever capacity or relationships the social genius of humanity demands such organization. To say that the spiritual unity is necessarily furthered by manifold social division would seem to be an inverse mode of thinking. It would seem that if we really can, on the basis of our common faith in a common Lord, approach each other, it would steadily diminish divisive tendencies and, by comprehending all that is vital and eliminating all that is nonessential, come to be more united in external organization, and so by a great example testifying to the world the unifying power and fundamental adaptability of Christianity for its work as a universal religion.''

THE NEW CRUSADE

We hail with joy the dawning of that good day when strife and discord shall die out of the world, after having first died out of the Christian Church.

> "A sweeter song shall then be heard,
> The music of the world's accord,
> Confessing Christ the inward word.
>
> That song shall stretch from shore to shore;
> Our faith, our hope, our love restore
> The seamless robe which Jesus wore."

III

There is the ceaseless crusade for Democracy.

There exists between autocracy and democracy an opposition so fundamental that all compromise is impossible. Autocracy sets up a government without the consent of the governed. Autocracy professes to rule by divine right, and affirms the personal irresponsibility of the king. Autocracy claims that man exists for the State. Autocracy proceeds by overhead authority. Autocracy becomes cruel and exercises the policy of frightfulness, because too much power is lodged in the hands of a few.

On the other hand democracy, according to the well-known words of Lincoln, is "government of the people, by the people, and for the people."

Again he says: "No man is good enough or

wise enough to govern another man without his consent."

Mazzini says: "Democracy is the progress of all, through all, under the leadership of the best and the wisest."

Lowell says: "Democracy is that form of society in which every man has a chance and knows that he has."

According to the Declaration of Independence it is an equal right "to life, liberty, and the pursuit of happiness." The very heart of democracy is its purpose to give to all equality of opportunity, with the recognition that men are unequal in capacity. The main purpose of Carlyle in "Sartor Resartus" is to show this essential equality of man, when stripped of material and external habiliments.

Democracy is the form of society which is in harmony with the nature of man and is therefore God's plan of human government.

Democracy has nothing in common with the mad folly of Bolshevism. Bolshevism, like autocracy, is class legislation and class rule.

It is another case in which extremes meet— Bolshevism is autocracy on the part of the ignorant and unwashed and unshaved. Irresponsible autocracy produces Bolshevism as in Russia. Democracy is our only safeguard against Bolshevism. Democracy must win its way against the opposition of both autocracy and Bolshevism.

Autocracy recognizes no authority beyond itself. Its power is spontaneous, intrinsic, and inherent. It relies on force. It demands isolation for safety. It shuts out the vulgar from the presence of the would-be-great. Autocrats in their own esteem are of bluer blood and finer clay than the common people. Autocracy claims the right to deceive the people, since in reality they have no right to know. If deceiving the people leads to a larger measure of security, then there is no scruple as to the deception. It necessarily leads to cruelty, since aloofness and snobbery destroy human compassion.

In a democracy the masses of the people participate in government. All authority is a trust. In practice the many are always ruled by the few, but the many claim the right to select the few.

Democracy rests on faith. It believes that men may be trusted. It demands equality before the law and equality before the bar of justice. It results in the dominance of public opinion over the autocratic notions of a select coterie.

A necessary element in democracy is a sense of duty and responsibility. You cannot make a democracy out of people who are forever thinking of their rights and never of their responsibilities.

A recent writer says: "Democracy has two great enemies, the demagogue and the cynic." The demagogue inflames the passions and prejudices of men; the cynic denies all possibility of progress and improvement.

Dr. J. H. Snowden writes: "More and more our civilization is exalting the worth of human personality from the top to the bottom of society. It is this sense of the supreme value of personality that has struck the fetters from the slaves, elevated women, and is throwing protection around the child. The worth of simple personality is being raised above the ancient rights of property. It is this that brought thrones and crowns crashing down in the great war. Democracy asserted itself against despotism, and personality against brute power. It is this value of the human personality that is dissolving and leveling special privileges and social distinctions of royalty and nobility and wealth and is flooding the world with democracy."

No less a personage than Jesus Christ is responsible for democracy. He exercised the most implicit faith in the potentialities of the common man. He ignored the external distinctions of class and caste. His Church, through all her imperfections, has been the one and only organization that has received into her ranks the rich and poor, the learned and unlearned, with a peni-

THE NEW CRUSADE

tent heart as the one requirement of all. It is in harmony with the genius of Christianity that our government, political and ecclesiastical, shall be broad-based on the will of the people.

Democracy came first in religion in the common man's demand that he shall be his own priest before God. It comes next in politics in the demand of men that they shall have a voice in determining what their government shall be. It comes last in industry in the demand of men that they shall have something to say about the conditions under which they shall work.

There is the sixfold manifestation of democracy in State, education, freedom of speech, industry, in church, and in religion.

IV

Growing out of the Crusade for Democracy is the Crusade for Social Betterment.

The Church with the false individualistic philosophy has been responsible for the reeking filth of entire communities and the loss of multitudes of souls. We have dealt in our miserable half-truths, which are worse in effect than lies. The half-truth is more dangerous than a whole falsehood. The half-truth has enough truth to give carrying power to the error.

"A lie which is all a lie may be met and fought with outright;
But a lie which is half a truth is a harder matter to fight."

Take, for example, "Clean up a man's soul and he will clean up his own premises." It has happened in almost numberless instances that drunken bums have stumbled into a gospel mission, and through the saving power of the gospel have gone out to live a decent and a religious life. Our lopsided individualist then proceeds to the fallacy of maintaining that this is to be the sole and only method for solving the physical wretchedness of people. He is willing to allow submerged populations to rot in filth and disease and spread their contagion while he indulges the half-truth. "The soul of improvement is the improvement of the soul." But it is not the sole improvement. How manifestly true it is that in a large number of instances the total improvement of the person must begin on the plane of the physical; he must be cleaned up before any latent self-respect is awakened, and his environment must either be changed or he must be taken out of his environment.

It is the inescapable duty of the Church to minister in a constructive way and in the way of permanent helpfulness to the physical wretchedness of people. Again it is very agreeable to the individualistic churchman to "think below his diaphragm" in order to protect his dividends.

A true program of social betterment calls for a high venture and the risk of high expenditures, although in the long run, if the self-interest of the individualist were not too blind to see it, it is a good financial proposition.

There should be a strict regulation of the sanitary conditions of tenement structures. The decent portion of society should say to the great unwashed throng, "Your individual liberty has already reached the vanishing point; you may not be free, but water is free, and if necessary we will furnish the soap, because soap is cheap, and there is no such thing as a sanitary room with unsanitary people in it."

The decent part of society should say, "We are not dealing in soft sentiment. If you are not willing to clean up, you can exercise the remnant of liberty that is left you by living out in the open, and we will put your children in healthful surroundings; and we are willing to do this because the cost to society will be less than a new crop of criminals."

And at last this will do more than anything else to start a real revival of religion among this element of our population.

It will also serve to remove our false fatalism in theology that a high death rate is the predestined provision of an inscrutable Providence.

Modern science has made clear the direct relation between physical and spiritual welfare. Poor eyesight in the child has been mistaken for dullness and indifference. A social worker told me an incident of having glasses fitted to the eyes of a little daughter of a factory operative, who looked around with an unearthly rapture on her face and exclaimed: "O Miss Nan, I can see." The presence of adenoids has been mistaken for indwelling demons.

Bad housing conditions and lack of recreational facilities in the crowded sections of the submerged have led boys and girls into sin and a criminal career, while comfortable churchmen solved the problem by an appeal to their Scriptural doctrine of total depravity.

Bishop C. W. Burns sounds the advancing note: "This is the day for the prophet to be the advance herald of the new social order that for old heresy proclaims new faith, for old mirages of blindness new programs of social betterment. With hearts throbbing to the reveille of the future, let the prophets of God advance. Out yonder where the enemy is intrenched, where social wrongs and industrial injustice are rampant; where life is hurt and cramped and crowded; where happiness is blighted, where moral purpose is robbed of purity, where wretchedness is focused; where might is braggart and shiftlessness is sullen; where vice entices at every corner and is intrenched in the liberty of license; where holy impulse is stifled, where hope gutters down like a candle in its socket, where love is stricken dead on altars of devotion; out where tyranny is the blight and sarcoma of the race; where Bolshevism rears its ogre head; where the fight of the Kingdom is thickest; where the Christ calls—lead on, O prophets of the dawning day."

Jesus Christ is forever the champion of the weak.

> "Therefore he went
> And humbly joined himself to the weaker part,
> So he could be the nearer to God's heart
> And feel its solemn pulse sending blood
> Through all the widespread veins of endless good."

V

There is the Crusade for National Welfare and Unity.

A distinct contribution in the teaching of Jesus was his estimate of men above institutions. Not only are the Sabbath and the Church constituted for man, but the State exists for the welfare of the people. Since the State, however, is composed of people, the ideal of the individual citizen is to be the mutual welfare of all the citizens.

There are certain perils which beset us to-day against which we must carry on a truceless warfare.

1. A perennial stream of immigrants pours into the United States, which is straining the capacity of the melting pot.

There are in the United States 14,000,000 people who are foreign born and 22,000,000 of foreign parentage. More than 150 different languages and dialects are spoken, and more than 1,300 foreign-language newspapers are published with a circulation of more than 10,000,000.

There are 2,500,000 adult foreigners who cannot speak our language.

In the process of assimilation there should be the requirement that every foreign newspaper should carry a parallel column in English. The children of foreigners should be compelled to learn English. Children readily respond in loyalty to American ideals. The story is told of a boy of foreign-born parentage who objected to parental chastisement on the ground that he objected to being whipped by a foreigner. A further aid to assimilation is the encouragement to foreigners to buy property for residence purposes. The public school and the evangelizing work of the Churches are potent factors in the process of Americanization. But with all the efforts toward assimilation, our government should exercise the right of a reasonable restriction on immigration.

2. The peril of the liquor traffic should call forth the uncompromising opposition of every patriotic citizen. The most powerful and unscrupulous foe of our American institutions is the organized liquor forces. The basis of this power is not in the appetite of the weak individ-

ual, but in the organized greed of liquor dealers who are willing to murder the bodies and souls of their victims for gain. With the sophistry of personal liberty, they would burden society with their wreckage of pauperism, crime, and insanity. This dragon of darkness must be met by the organized forces of the Church, with the realization that it is a war to the death and one or the other must go down.

3. Intellectual and spiritual illiteracy is an enemy to national welfare and unity.

In 1920 there were in the United States 4,931,905 illiterates. Six per cent of the entire population over ten years of age had received no schooling whatever. The first draft in the recent war disclosed the startling fact that one-fourth of the young men called to the colors could neither read nor write. Their average mental age was about fourteen.

Of the 42,000,000 children and youth in the United States under twenty-five years of age who are Protestant or nominally Protestant, 27,000,000 are unreached by the educational program of any Church. The only remedy is in the State making school attendance compulsory either in public, private, or Church schools, and in the Church carrying on a continual crusade for new Sunday school pupils, and the fostering of higher institutions of learning on which we are dependent for instructors.

4. There is the growing peril resulting from the extremes of wealth and poverty.

We have too large a number in our country who live without working, and too large a number who work without living. We have hundreds of idle rich who waste far more than would be sufficient to feed hundreds who are starving. The peril of corporate greed is in producing the reaction of wild radicalism and revolution. The old Bourbon idea of the sole comfort of the upper class has passed.

This distinction was expressed in the cringing prayer of the poor:

> "God bless the Squire and all his rich relations,
> And teach us poor folks to keep our stations."

But with the spread of democratic ideals any inequality of human conditions which is the result of injustice and the selfish accumulation of wealth will prove a constant irritation and disturbance in our social life.

Personal values must be placed above property values. John Ruskin was a pioneer in the advocacy of this high principle of Jesus when he contended that the wealth of a nation is to be estimated by the number of healthy, moral, and happy human beings who compose it. The most neglected child in any back alley or dingy street of your city is worth more than all your banks and piles of brick and stone. Property

THE NEW CRUSADE

has its rights, but the rights of humanity must take precedence. Human welfare is the first consideration. The people who are very much disturbed over a panic which destroys property values are able to bear with remarkable resignation the destruction of human values.

5. A final weakening influence which may be mentioned is the divisiveness of sectionalism.

It was the irreconcilable hot-heads on both sides in our nation who were responsible for the bloody strife between brothers. The same kind of citizens who try to keep alive the fires of enmity between the sections of our country are the same kind of citizens as those who precipitated the war.

In a city in one of our most distinctively Southern States there is inscribed on a monument: "Forever in the past is sacrifice, in the future progress. One hundred years ago the men of the North and South fought together. One people—No North—No South—A common interest—One country—One destiny. As it was, so ever let it be."

The matchless Grady threw out the challenge of reconciliation to the North: "This hour little needs the loyalty that is loyal to one section and yet holds the other in enduring suspicion and estrangement. Give us the broad and perfect loyalty that loves and trusts Georgia alike with Massachusetts—that knows no South, no

North, no East, no West, but endears with equal and patriotic love every foot of our soil, every State of our Union."

But with all that may be said we must rely primarily on spiritual agencies for our national welfare and unity.

Our own nation could not continue for a decade without religion and the Christian Churches.

I do not wish to give any suggestion of special pleading, but no man can be in the truest significance a patriot who does not live in loyalty to those religious principles which alone are the safeguard of a nation.

The average American loves to sing:

> "My country, 'tis of thee,
>   Sweet land of liberty,
>   Of thee I sing:
> Land where my fathers died,
> Land of the pilgrims' pride,
> From every mountain side
>   Let freedom ring."

But the singer is only dealing in the rhythm of words unless he can sing in the faith and in the spirit:

> "Our fathers' God, to thee,
>   Author of liberty
>   To thee we sing;
> Long may our land be bright
> With freedom's holy light;
> Protect us by thy might,
>   Great God, our King."

Patriotism is not dealing in empty jingoism.

Patriotism is not preaching a selfish and narrow Americanism.

Patriotism is not making a noise on the Fourth of July.

Patriotism is not proud of mere material prosperity.

Patriotism is not boastful of American superiority.

Patriotism is not canonizing dead heroes and statesmen.

Patriotism is not pandering to class prejudice and passion.

Patriotism recognizes that we are traitors to the State unless we endeavor to the best of our understanding to exercise our suffrage for good men, good laws, and good government.

Patriotism recognizes that only "Righteousness exalteth a people."

Patriotism is hearing the call of God and following the providential guidance of God amid the perplexing problems of our present day.

Patriotism is allegiance to the teachings of Jesus Christ, which alone can make our nation secure and great.

Patriotism is carrying our religious loyalty into all the practical affairs of government, that the worse elements that would bring danger to our national safety may be overcome.

"O beautiful for patriot dream
That sees beyond the years
Thine alabaster cities gleam,
Undimmed by human tears!
America! America!
God shed his grace on thee,
And crown thy good with brotherhood
From sea to shining sea."

CHAPTER X

THE NEW CRUSADE (Concluded)

VI

SINCE no nation can any longer live within itself and for itself, there follows the Crusade for Internationalism.

A large part of our ills has come from isolation, individualism, and provincialism. The bugbear of "entangling alliances" is no longer pertinent. When Washington spoke these words there were a few thousand people along the Atlantic coast. He had no conception of 100,000,000 people, with all the complex relationships of our modern world. Washington has been dead over a century, and if he should wake up in the United States to-day he would not know where he was. We have passed from stagecoaches to express trains, telephones, wireless telegraphy, submarines, and airships. There are guns that shoot farther than a man could ride in a day in Washington's time. Washington lived at least a twenty-days' voyage from Europe, while we are only twenty-four hours' distant, and London can be reached by cable or wireless in a few seconds.

Extreme nationalism gives rise to a dangerous provincial patriotism. There is no place in the heart of a true patriot for the popular oratorical motto, "My country, right or wrong." Our own constitution was nothing more originally than a league of independent States conscious of their weakness if standing apart.

The Church must make her influence felt, for the question of international relationship is not only a political but a brotherhood question.

A recent writer says: "If ever there was a time when the nations of the earth should prepare for peace instead of for war, now is the time. The whole question of disarmament practically lies in the hands of the two great Protestant, Christian nations, Great Britain and the United States. If they would agree to disarm, Japan would also, and the whole matter would be practically settled, for there are no other navies worth considering left. The cost of standing armies through the years has been infinitely more than the cost of education. To spend forty million dollars for a new battleship which can be blown out of the water by a flying machine that hardly costs forty thousand dollars is a piece of financial folly, to say nothing more. What this world wants to-day is a league of nations that will comprise all the governments, great and small, an international court, and just enough of police force on land and sea, supported by all the signatory governments to the league, to enforce the decisions of the court. All this could easily be accomplished if our lawmakers at Washington had the Christian viewpoint instead of the viewpoint of the party politician. Petty politics have all but destroyed the respect of the nations for the United States."

An international alliance for the preservation of world order is the goal toward which the world is inevitably moving, and political standpatters and reactionaries may delay, but they cannot defeat, the movement. It is the clear call of Christ.

> "In the years that have been I have bound man closer to man
>   And closer woman to woman;
> And the stranger hath seen in a stranger his brother at last
>   And a sister in eyes that were strange.
> In the years that shall be I will bind me nation to nation
>   And shore unto shore, saith our God.
> Lo, I am the burster of bonds and the breaker of barriers;
> I am he that shall free, saith the Lord.
> For the lingering battle, the contest of ages is ending,
>   And victory followeth me."

VII

Linked with the Crusade for Internationalism is the Crusade for World Peace.

There are some considerations which should meet with response from reasonable people. There are those who would muddy the stream of clear thinking. The issue is not between a theoretic pacifism and increased military preparedness. The question is, in this day of peace with the wisdom that should come from experience, what should be our attitude toward war and what should be our efforts toward universal peace?

1. War must be stripped of its false glory. It must be seen in its undisguised hideousness and horror. We must cease to idealize war. Sentimental women who think that a brass button on a bright uniform is perfectly lovely should see the torn uniform and the mangled body and the brass buttons soiled with mud and stained with blood.

We must not forget the bitter lessons of the past. Lloyd George recently said: "The old generation is passing away, and a new generation that knows nothing of the terror and discomfort of the Great War will be drenched by historians, novelists, and artists with a description of its glories."

2. The double standard of morality as applied to nations and individuals must be condemned. Why should individuals be held to a tribunal of justice for settlement of disputes, while nations are held to be justifiable in resorting to uncontrolled passion and violence?

The nation that refuses to abide by the international law should be treated by the other nations as a policeman would deal with an obstreperous individual.

3. War must not be regarded as a permanent institution. There has always existed the rigidly conservative type who regards any existent evil as forever fixed. It was true in the case of dueling, polygamy, slavery, and piracy. It is the blackest pessimism to regard war as permanently intrenched in human society.

When a shipment of American boys killed in the World War was unloaded on the Hoboken pier, President Harding looked out over literally acres of boxes containing all that remained of potential builders of civilization, and said with deep feeling: "This must not be again."

The Methodist Episcopal Church sent out this notable utterance: "Millions of our fellow men have died heroically in 'a war to end war.' What they undertook, we must finish by methods of peace. War is not inevitable. It is the supreme enemy of mankind. Its futility is beyond question. Its continuance is the suicide of civilization. We are determined to outlaw the whole war system.

"The patriotism of the Methodist Episcopal Church has never been challenged. Neither our motives nor our loyalty must be impugned when we insist on the fulfillment of pledges made to the dead and assert our Christian ideals for the living. Governments which ignore the Christian conscience of men in time of peace cannot justly claim the lives of men in time of war.

Secret diplomacy and political partisanship must not draw men into the dilemma of deciding between support of country and loyalty to Christ.

"The world is now open to a crusade for peace. War-weary nations everywhere are eagerly waiting. America must lead the way. Our nation and our Church can do now what we may never be able to do again."

4. The race of military preparedness does not stop war. America should lead the way to an international agreement, which gives notice to any belligerent nation that when it breaks forth into violence it encounters the opposition of the other nations combined. When nations prepare for war, they will precipitate war.

5. The people should demand of their government that questions in dispute must be settled by some other method than the appeal to the brutality of war. It is estimated that fewer than twenty men brought on the late war. The blundering leaders who bring on war always manage to keep their own hides whole.

6. War is the chief handicap to the progress of humanity. War is the devouring monster that swallows up ninety-three cents out of every dollar of taxation. The money spent on war would build churches and schoolhouses in reach of every human being, turn the waste places of the earth into a garden, and relieve a large part of the woes that afflict mankind.

THE NEW CRUSADE

7. Another world war would mean universal carnage and destruction. It would involve the wholesale slaughter of armies and cities. Inventions such as poison gas, devices for the spread of disease germs, and the "death ray" reveal very plainly that the future holds in store nothing less than the complete downfall of civilization and the suicide of humanity, unless the forces of Christianity can overtake and bring under rational and moral control the conscienceless materialism that stalks threateningly among the nations in this very hour.

If an international agreement fails, then please remember that your military preparedness cannot proceed along the old methods. The main line of preparation would necessarily be the construction of huge aëroplanes and the production of poisonous gases. After the invention of gunpowder, there were doubtless medieval knights who wanted to keep on fighting the old way, but after smelling gunpowder a few times they decided to change their method.

8. The sane Christian course for the United States to pursue is to join the other nations in laying a foundation for enduring peace. The old motto, as false as it is old, "In time of peace prepare for war," must be changed to "In time of peace prepare for peace." When the war clouds gather it will be too late to think clearly and rationally. It is the supreme duty of the

United States to think in terms of peace, to hold forth the ideal of peace, and to lead the nations out of the hellish war system.

It is nothing short of criminal to talk war unless our government does the utmost to accomplish this high mission and then fails.

9. In our Crusade for Peace we have the encouragement of a powerful peace sentiment which is many times stronger than ever before. Wherever the Church has spoken as a group, it has been against the military mania. The Federal Council of Churches makes a statement of the "Creed for Believers in a Warless World":

WE BELIEVE in a sweeping reduction of armaments.

WE BELIEVE in international law, courts of justice, and boards of arbitration.

WE BELIEVE in a world-wide association of nations for world peace.

WE BELIEVE that Christian patriotism demands the practice of good will between nations.

WE BELIEVE that nations no less than individuals are subject to God's immutable moral laws.

WE BELIEVE that nations that are Christian have special international obligations.

WE BELIEVE in a warless world and dedicate ourselves to its achievement.

> "Let friendly flags be far unfurled,
> Be hushed the quarrel of the world.
> God's leaders can no more afford
> The pagan swagger with the sword.
> War attitudes but anger men,
> And make them burn to fight again.

By love and truth must men grow great,
And live to put war out of date.
Let armaments dissolve with rust,
And let mad sabers waste in dust.
White hands of peace in this new day
Must wash the stains of war away.''

VIII

The crowning consummation of all the aspiring and striving of the Christian heart for a true world order is the Crusade for the Kingdom of God on Earth.

The Kingdom of God is the great term which Jesus uses more than any other. He uses it eight times in the Sermon on the Mount and one hundred and twelve times in the four gospels. The larger number of the parables are parables of the kingdom. He commissioned the twelve and seventy to preach the gospel of the kingdom. It was the first and last note of his own preaching.

"By the kingdom of God is meant an ideal social order in which the relation of men to God is that of sons, and to each other that of brothers."

There are some three distinct errors as regards the kingdom:

1. It has been assumed by the strict individualist that the kingdom of God is identical with the heaven of the future. The goal of the gospel

is accomplished when the individual soul makes his way through this present evil world into the sinless future realm.

2. The error that the kingdom is identical with the visible Church is the tenet of the Roman Catholic Church. The Roman papacy, with a political conception of the kingdom, accomplished for more than one thousand years some of the wonders of history. Pope Gregory VII compels Henry IV of Germany to stand outside the palace at Canossa for three days in the cold of January in penitential garb, beseeching audience of the Pope. Frederick I, the stalwart German emperor, holds the stirrup of Pope Adrian IV at Rome and prostrates himself on the stone pavement at Venice before Pope Alexander III. Pope Innocent III brings Philip Augustus of France to subjection and compels King John of England to surrender his crown and dominions. Frederick II of Germany dies heartbroken under the shadow of a defeat inflicted by Pope Innocent IV.

This theory of the identity of a visible Church with the kingdom of God has received too many hard blows to survive in its pristine strength, and the voice of the Vatican is now the echo of an echo.

3. The third error is that the kingdom of God is the visible reign of Christ in millennial glory. It is a Jewish survival based on apocalyptic

literature. Jesus tells us nothing of a thousand years' visible reign of Christ on earth.

The favorite book of Adventism is Revelation, along with some Old Testament prophecies, and their marvelous interpretation of these Scriptures is mixed in one jumble.

A literal passage which does not suit their purpose they make figurative, and a figurative passage they will make literal if thereby it suits their purpose better. They bewail the lack of spirituality of both the common saint and the Biblical scholar who cannot exclaim "crystal" when they propound their theory.

Prof. Shirley Jackson Case says: "The quintessence of religion is made to consist in assent to the fanciful millennial program, and those Christians who refuse such assent are assigned to the outer court. To inaugurate any program of social betterment or to set the Church as a whole upon an upward course would be to thwart the divine purpose and to delay the coming of Christ. Both the world and the Church must grow constantly worse in order to meet premillennial ideals."

There is the depreciation of all efforts for world peace through a league of nations. The success of peace plans would contradict their theory; therefore they can only prophesy war, if not hope for it, until the second advent. One writer says: "We talk of disarmament, but we all know that it is not coming." All our present peace plans will end in the most awful wars and conflicts the old world ever saw.

The missionary enterprise is to be carried on, but not with the expectation that the world is to be won for Christ. Dr. Haldeman, in the *Sunday School Times*, says: "The rallying cry of Protestantism, 'the world for Christ,' is a false slogan." Another periodical says: "We are not to preach the gospel of the kingdom, or even to pray for its extension, for the kingdom cannot even commence until the Lord comes."

Compared with premillennialists, Schopenhauer is a radiant optimist. In opposition to such hopelessness we must be on our guard against an easy-going optimism. During the persecution of Jews in Russia some years ago, when hundreds were being slain, it was reported in the daily papers that Andrew Carnegie sent them a telegram saying, "Do not be discouraged. Under the law of evolution we must steadily, though slowly, march upward, and finally reach the true conception of the brotherhood of man." This message, it is needless to say, was not very comforting.

The only way to meet the deepest need of the human heart at all times and especially in times of great calamity, when the catastrophic idea makes such an appeal to the popular imagination, is to proclaim a gospel so full of vitality

THE NEW CRUSADE

and assurance and power that men will no longer feel the need of a cataclysmic method.

Jesus expected his gospel to succeed through the invisible spiritual agencies that are operative in the world. The program of Jesus is in the Great Commission, which the Premillennialists are very shy about quoting: "All power is given unto me in heaven and in earth. Go ye therefore, and make disciples of all the nations, baptizing them in the name of the Father, and of the Son, and of the Holy Spirit; teaching them to observe all things whatsoever I have commanded you; and lo, I am with you alway, even unto the end of the world."

The gospel is a revelation of the saving power of God as revealed in Christ for all human relations. It is not pessimistic about humanity. It knows that the world, despite sinful men, is becoming better, because it is growing more loyal to justice and love. It looks across the range of history from the Stone Age to the present world order and sees satisfactory progress toward the ideals of Jesus Christ. Those who thus use the Bible believe that the moral principles of Jesus are actually to be operative in history because of God's working in Christian men living in the Spirit of Jesus. They make central the teachings of Jesus as to God and morals rather than views of pre-Christian Judaism. They believe the kingdom of God will come by the spiritual transformation of human society, and that it is already coming. Such a use of the Scripture does not separate Christianity from the growing knowledge of the universe and society given by science. In the place of diagrams and ingenious fulfillments of prophecy, it sees a universe filled with a God of law and love.

Dr. W. N. Clarke says: "The kingdom of God that was really at hand when Jesus appeared has been developed in the existing order of this world's life. At present we can read the past plainly enough to see that this was the only right and possible method. There was nothing in the work of Jesus that tended to bring upon the world a miraculous catastrophe, and nothing in his influence for good that would have had its characteristic promotion in such an event. From the result it does not appear that he came to produce new heavens and a new earth, except as any place is new wherein dwells righteousness. In the normal successions of human history his work was wrought out in accordance with its nature. The appropriate result of a work like his was the long unfolding of the grace of God in the world. The kingdom of God that came in with Jesus was the practical dominion of God in the life that men live together—a kingdom that came, and is still coming, and has yet to come."

Dr. H. C. King writes: "This literalistic premillennialism is contrary to the whole spirit of the teaching of Christ, for it reveals an essentially atheistic disbelief in spiritual forces and repudiation of them, yielding to a temptation which Christ himself rejected in the wilderness struggle. Moreover, it practically sets aside the whole social aspect of the kingdom of God, and makes meaningless Christ's prayer, 'Thy kingdom come, Thy will be done on earth . . . ' "

In the darkest hour that ever cast its shadow on our sinful earth Jesus said: "This gospel of the kingdom shall be preached in all the world." To lose the spirit of hope is to lose the Spirit of Christ. He staked everything on the universality of his kingdom. This was the occasion of his death. The Jews were infuriated at the thought of a universal gospel. A universal gospel is made sacred by the baptism of his blood.

The man who opposes the universality of his kingdom arrays himself on the side of the Jews against Christ, and on the side of both Jews and pagans against the early Church.

Tradition tells us that two Roman emperors were willing to admit the image of the Christ in the pantheon as the equal of other gods. But the Christians would have no partial honor bestowed upon their Lord. Jesus tolerates no rival authority in religion. His authority is to be all-exclusive and his kingdom is to be all-inclusive. There can be but one sun in the heavens. Our Lord shall not see of the travail of his soul and be satisfied until, with liberal hands and with devoted lives, the Christian Church makes possible the kingdom of God on earth.

> "Jesus shall reign where'er the sun
> Does his successive journeys run;
> His kingdom spread from shore to shore,
> Till moons shall wax and wane no more."

The declaration of Prof. C. A. Ellwood is in harmony with the words of this old hymn and with the purpose of Jesus. "Christianity is an endeavor to establish a world-wide, ideal human society in which justice and good will shall be realized upon a religious basis."

It is Jesus Christ for the world or nothing.

Men will not leave him for a lower form of religion and they will never have a chance for a higher form. To turn away from Christ is to turn away from the hope of life. Even Renan says: "Whatever may be the surprises of the future, Jesus will never be surpassed."

There can be no higher law than the law of love.

There can be no higher truth than the Fatherhood of God. There can be no more universal principle than the brotherhood of man. There can be no higher righteousness than the complete inner and outer transformation of life that belongs to the Christian faith.

There can be no higher exemplification of the brotherhood of man than the example of Christ.

There can be no stronger power for righteousness than the power that comes from an obedient relationship to Jesus Christ.

Since the Christian faith is the most valuable possession of a human life, every high motive that belongs to the Christian spirit impels us to share the priceless treasure, to share our best with those who are poor without it.

This is a day when we ought to be ashamed to take a provincial view of life. The universalizing of Christianity is the one work that clearly rests upon the conception of the brotherhood of all men in Christ, of whatever land and clime. Lord Bryce has said: "The one sure hope for a permanent foundation of world peace lies in the expansion throughout the world of the principles of the Christian gospel."

All the centuries circle around Jesus Christ, and unto him all nations, tribes, and peoples shall finally come. It is God's decree that every knee shall bow to him, and every tongue confess that he is King of Kings and Lord of Lords.

The glorious crusade before the Christian Church is the Crusade for World Christianity.

We are at first startled when our attention is called to the fact of the comparatively small amount of the teaching of Jesus which has to do with immortality and heaven and we are surprised to discover that he has more than twice as much to say about the earth as he has to say about heaven. What Jesus does say about these eternal realities is sufficient and he has no disposition to minimize them, but his wisdom in placing emphasis on the kingdom of God on earth is justified, when we see how the Church has been prone to minimize it.

We have actually taken the inspired forecast of the kingdom of God on earth and transferred it by false interpretation to heaven. The prophet of Patmos sees a new order on a new earth. "And I John saw the holy city, new Jerusalem, coming down from God out of heaven. . . . And I heard a great voice out of heaven saying, Behold, the tabernacle of God is with men, and he will dwell with them, and they shall be his people, and God himself shall be with them, and be their God."

The immortal spirits of the saints in light must be thrilled with a new rapture at every triumph of the kingdom of God on earth; and whether or not the new earth will at last be the habitation of all the redeemed spirits, yet heaven will be more glorious when the kingdom of God is fully set up on the new earth.

> "Then shall all men's good
> Be each man's rule, and universal Peace
> Lie like a shaft of light across the land."

Toward this realization we are not to exercise an easy-going optimism with a credulity that believes in the omnipotence of mere processes and drifts and tendencies, but with hearts strengthened by the hope of Christ we are to dedicate to him the unreserved devotion and sacrificial loyalty of our lives. When we reckon with the greed and selfishness of men with its harvest of wretchedness and hate, we can but think of our own generation as "the ancients of the earth and in the morning of the times."

But there is the abiding hopefulness of the gospel. This hope is to persist against all discouragement and to rejoice in the better day that is coming to the world. We cannot say how far, but somewhere in the far future our faith tells us that this crowning day is coming.

With a faith in the unfailing mission of Jesus Christ, we shall find ourselves in accord with the prophecy of Prof. John Fiske: "The future is lighted for us with the radiant colors of hope. Strife and sorrow shall disappear. Peace and love shall reign supreme. The dream of poets, the lesson of priest and prophet, the inspiration of the great musician, is confirmed in the light of modern knowledge; and as we gird ourselves up for the work of life, we may look forward to the time when in the truest sense the kingdoms of this world shall become the kingdom of Christ, and he shall reign forever and ever, King of Kings and Lord of Lords."

There yet remain many steep ascents through peril, toil, and pain, but some glad day a redeemed humanity, the perfect consummation of the kingdom of God on earth, will be the reward of the perfect sacrifice of Jesus Christ.

WITHDRAWN
from
Funderburg Library